GW00992353

Ian Martin is married with two children and lives in North East Wales. He is a Royal Navy veteran having served on *HMS Ark Royal* and *HMS London* during the first Gulf War. He was diagnosed with a neuro-muscular condition in 1994 and medically discharged from the Navy. For the last 20 years he has played a leading role in developing the sport of cricket for people with disabilities, becoming the England and Wales Cricket Board's first full-time Disability Manager in 2007. He has led 17 overseas cricket tours and overseen the growth in participation of disabled people in cricket to over 70,000 people. He is a Trustee of the Lord's Taverners and The Neuro-Muscular Centre in Winsford, Cheshire. Ian is a member of The Marylebone Cricket Club and is a season ticket holder at Everton Football Club.

To Joanna, Conor & Ciara: thank you for supporting me to pursue my dream and for everything that is good in my life, keeping me grounded and making me laugh. You are my world.

To Paul Cartwright, thanks; you know what for.

To my brother Paul, Aunty Pat & Uncle Kenny and Uncle Brian for all of your love, support and understanding.

Thanks to the staff and clients of the Neuro-Muscular Centre in Winsford for helping me make sense of my disability and for endless support and advice on dealing with it.

To Rich, Bradders and his deviant digit, Bobby, Kitchen, Gaz, Scotty, Hights, Martin, Degs, Flowers, Mr Peter, Cooky, Ross, Stu, Edgar, Bill, Qas, Fran, Emma, Box, Dayle and Ellers – thanks for giving me the best support on and off the field and for so many great nights.

Finally, to Jason & Jenny, Carron & Steve and Tim & Tracey for the parties, love and support.

Ian Martin

HOW CRICKET SAVED MY LIFE

AUSTIN MACAULEY PUBLISHERS™

LONDON * CAMBRIDGE * NEW YORK * SHARJAH

A CIP catalogue record for this title is available from the British Library.

ISBN 9781398451414 (Paperback)
ISBN 9781398451421 (Hardback)
ISBN 9781398451438 (ePub e-book)

www.austinmacauley.com

First Published 2022
Austin Macauley Publishers Ltd®
1 Canada Square
Canary Wharf
London
E14 5AA

To all who have helped me make this book possible and encouraged me to continue with it: Clare Connor CBE, Hannah Murphy, Brian Newbury, Roger Meredith, Matthew Lanham, Richard Hill MBE, Suzy Christopher, Chris Haynes.

Thanks to all at Austin Macauley for believing in me and allowing my story to be told.

Foreword for Ian's Book

Whilst this might not be a traditional cricket book, Ian Martin certainly has cricket coursing through his veins. I have worked alongside Ian at the England & Wales Cricket Board for over a decade and have witnessed his devotion to the advancement of disability cricket grow stronger and stronger during that time. Why such devotion? Because cricket saved Ian. And now cricket sustains him and drives him.

In the early pages of this book you will meet a fit, physically active, brave, competitive young man with a career of active military service stretching ahead of him. A young man serving his country in Her Majesty's Royal Navy and experiencing active service during the first Gulf War. A team player. A young man determined to make his family proud by absorbing new experiences, taking on new challenges and doing his best. A young man with no sense of limitation. But this young man returned home from months at sea, to a diagnosis of a physically degenerative condition. Hereditary yes, but possibly made worse by medication he received whilst serving in the Gulf.

A burgeoning career in the Navy was abruptly and cruelly taken away and so this young man was forced to take stock and forge a new path. And my goodness, did he find the right one.

As you read this book, I think you will find yourselves asking some complex questions about the relationship between luck – good and bad – and life choices and fulfilment. And about what it means to find your calling and your purpose. I know from the privileged position of working with Ian, that nobody could have devoted so many years of their life to a cause with any more passion and care and resilience than Ian has given to the cause of disability cricket.

What happened to Ian was undoubtedly cruel. He lost a huge amount when his diagnosis became clear. But he wasn't diminished by it – indeed the opposite happened. He directed his own loss and his own physical disability to make the sport better, kinder and more inclusive for others with disabilities. During his 20 years of ongoing service, Ian has created countless opportunities for cricketers with disabilities to travel the world, to be part of a team, to represent their country – just as he did when he set out as a 16 year old looking for adventure and belonging on HMS Ark Royal and HMS London.

This is a book about the power of sport and the power of family. Perhaps most importantly, it is a book about the power of purpose. I hope you enjoy reading it as much as I did.

Clare Connor CBE
Managing Director England Women's Cricket
President of The Marylebone Cricket Club (MCC) from October 2021

I've only known Ian Martin for a relatively short period of time. I joined the ECB as Managing Director of men's cricket in January 2019 and it was soon after that I started to bump into Ian either in the ECB offices at Lord's or in the Danubius hotel, situated across the road from the world's greatest cricket ground, where we'd both stay on occasion to save on the long commute both of us were making from our respective homes. At first it was a nod, a good morning or how you doing? However, in no time our conversations were much longer and more meaningful than that, and you only have to read a couple of chapters of this book to know why.

Ian is a truly extraordinary man. Someone who has faced incredible challenges in life, in work and in sport and yet continues to keep driving forward, dusting himself down after any setback and going again. That's not to say that Ian hasn't had some really difficult and low moments, and how could he not given some of the cards he's been dealt. However, I'm a great believer that it's not those moments that define any of us, it's how you deal with them. For me, that's what makes Ian extraordinary. This book is an amazing, honest and emotional account of Ian's life so far. In parts it's hard to read, and difficult to understand how anyone could cope with such adversity. Unsurprisingly, to those who know Ian, he meets all these challenges head on with an unbelievable passion for life, his family and the game of cricket.

Ian now reports into me on all area of performance disability cricket and so I get to experience his passion on a daily basis. I feel lucky to have Ian as part of my senior management team. He brings a different and important perspective to my team built on the rich and often difficult experiences he has had. He also has a very sharp sense of humour, which always goes down well in my teams.

Ian demonstrates a near super human determination in everything he commits to or volunteers for, always putting others needs and concerns before his own. He's had an incredible impact on disability cricket in this country in the twenty plus years he has been involved, and continues every day to push for greater equality for those with less access and opportunity to watch, play and enjoy cricket. In fact, I think it's fair to say, all cricket is better for Ian's involvement and the role he has played in driving change, not just disability cricket.

Ashley Giles MBE
Former Managing Director England Men's Cricket

Table of Contents

Prologue
Being Mankaded by the Navy

(Mankad – when a batsman is run out at the non-striker's end by the bowler. Often viewed as unsporting behaviour)

28th February 1994, Royal Navy Hospital Haslar, Gosport

I marched into, what I would describe as, an old, austere room that had seen years of Naval history. RNH Haslar predated Nelson and its wards had looked after casualties from every war since. Oak-panelled walls and bookshelves, and three senior naval surgeon officers, identified by the red bands between the gold braid on the sleeves of their jackets, sat behind a huge desk. I saluted and they told me to stand at ease. I remember thinking *that's easy for you to say, your career isn't on the line.*

That said, I'd woken that morning not for a moment thinking that I was going to be discharged from the Navy. My voice was a little hoarse as I'd made the trip south the day before via Villa Park, where I watched the League Cup Semi-final's 2nd Leg between Aston Villa and Tranmere Rovers. I was really unconcerned about my meeting at Haslar the following day. OK, so I'd been diagnosed with a condition that was certainly going to curtail my Service, but I was in a desk job, I'd passed my professional exams to become a Petty Officer, and I wasn't due to go back to sea for around eight years. I held Enhanced Positive Vetting, obtained at considerable cost to the Navy and afforded to very few in my line of work, which cleared me to work in the most Top-Secret places in the UK. In my mind, there was no way they would kick me out just yet. In my naïve mind, this meeting was a mere formality to let me know that they would review my situation, and I'd be back on the road north in no time to continue my life.

The more senior of the three officers, sat in the middle of them, began to review my Naval Career to date. "Joined aged 16 as a Junior Seaman, trained as a radar operator, two years on HMS Ark Royal with deployment to the Far East and Australia, promotion to Able Seaman and then retrained to become a Navy Writer. A quick return to sea onboard HMS London and Active Service during the Gulf War in 1990–91. Successful completion of security vetting and currently serving at a US Navy Unit in North East Scotland. Eight years Very Good conduct and Superior performance for the last three years"

Eight years of my life condensed into one neat paragraph. "You're a real asset to the Service, Martin," he continued.

"Thank You, sir," I replied. *This has all started well,* I thought. *A few more minutes and I'll be out of here.*

The Surgeon Commander continued, "But you've been diagnosed with Charcot Marie Tooth disease; do you understand what that means?" He continued before I could answer, "It means your muscle strength will deteriorate over time."

"I am fit to continue in my current role, Sir, and my Commanding Officer has requested that I be allowed to do so."

"As you know Martin, Her Majesties Royal Navy requires all personnel to be able to serve at sea at immediate notice. Tell me, do you think you could carry a stoker up a set of ladders out of a fire onboard ship?"

Stoker is the name given to the Navy's Marine Engineers. The term is usually prefixed with the descriptor "Hairy-Arsed", creating the, perhaps unfair, impression that they are all hairy, unfit and overweight grease monkeys.

Sensing that the conversation had taken a sharp alteration of course, I replied:

"Sir, in the normal course of the drafting cycle, I am not due to return to sea until the year 2002 and neither am I sure that the WRNS, who have recently gone to sea, could lift the same stoker to safety in the event of a fire onboard."

Not for the first or last time in my life, I knew the words coming out of my mouth were not helping my immediate cause. The MOD had only recently, within the previous three years, made the historical decision to allow the WRNS (Women's Royal Naval Service) to serve at sea. The decision had been overdue but was greeted by many within the Service with a great deal of scepticism. A lot of the older generation of sailors, and some of the younger ones, struggled to come to terms with it straight away. Strength to carry out some of the more labour-intensive tasks, such as the one I was being challenged with here, was one of the doubts raised by many of the old salts.

"Martin, do you wish to remain within the Service?" I was asked rather abruptly.

"Yes, sir," I replied. I couldn't believe he needed to ask.

"Very well, I note your request, but the decision will be made by an MOD Medical Board at Whitehall; you will be informed of its outcome by a signal to your Commanding Officer."

I saluted and marched towards the door. "Martin," I stopped in my tracks.

"Yes, Sir?"

"Don't build your hopes up." These were the last words he said to me before I left the room.

There was no discussion or reference made to whether the injections that I had been given during the Gulf War had any impact on my symptoms, and I wasn't given the opportunity to raise the question.

Distraught, devastated, disbelieving – it felt like I'd just been hit by a train. I couldn't take in what he had just said to me. I was in another world, completely dazed. I remember being taken into another room that was full of members of the Royal Navy Resettlement team. Their role was to advise people in my position of what amazing support the Navy offered to people leaving the service.

They had their work cut out with me that day because I was adamant that I wasn't leaving; I was in complete denial. I have no idea how long I was in there with them or how many different people advised me that I should at least give some thought to what might happen should I be discharged. I still have no idea, to this day, what support I was offered in that room because I never heard any of it.

I'd started the day thinking I was going to a meeting where the Navy was going to tell me how my newly diagnosed condition would be managed within the Service. By midday I was a wreck. Thinking back, as I write, I cannot believe how they even let me leave Haslar that day. I was mentally and emotionally distraught by what I had been told in that room which amounted to the following: "You're great at your job and you've done really well, an asset to the Service.

But you've got a disability now that's going to get worse as you get older.

We're not sure you're any use to us anymore.

We're probably gonna kick you out and make you redundant but we'll let your boss tell you in a few weeks' time".

My memory of the hours after the meeting with the Surgeon Commanders is non-existent. I don't know where I went or what I did. I remember getting back up to my base in Scotland a few days later and carrying on with work. Decision day at Whitehall was 15th March 1994.

In the intervening weeks, my Commanding Officer, Lieutenant Commander Graham Churton sent letters of appeal to all who would listen to state my case, even to ask for time before a decision was made to discharge me. I remember feeling quite confident that a sense of reason and fairness might be reached.

15 March 1994

We knew that the meeting in Whitehall would take place in the morning. By midday, we'd heard nothing; I was crawling up the walls, it was awful. In the end the boss sent me home. I was no use to anyone. By 4 pm, we still hadn't heard anything; it was unbearable. I drove back to the base; I took a hip flask full of rum and two shot glasses. The boss phoned Whitehall to find out what on earth was going on.

He came off the phone and said, "I'm sorry, its bad news." With five words my chosen career and my identity were gone. I took out the rum and poured us both a tot. I couldn't accept that I could be thrown onto a scrap heap at the age of 24.

Whilst I phoned my Mum, the boss called the rest of our small Royal Navy unit in the Communication Centre across the site and told them to finish early. By the time I'd come off the phone to Mum, the rest of our contingent had made their way over to the office that I shared with the boss. We were all in a state of disbelief, and I was holding back tears after explaining to Mum what had happened.

We headed over to the bar. I know I went through a bottle of Morgan's Spiced before we went into town that night. It never touched the sides. I was numb, completely devastated. I couldn't comprehend that I needed to make the transition back to being a civilian, and I really wasn't ready to try.

My diagnosis with CMT helped answer a lot of questions as well as raising a lot more, at least in my mind.

Dad had always struggled to walk properly for as long as I can remember. When my brother Paul and I were young, we would want to play football and cricket but Dad could never participate in the way that other Dads could. He would always take a shot at one of us in goal and then wobble and fall over.

When playing cricket, Dad never scored runs. He'd make his way between the wickets by what Paul and I used to call "fast walks". He would bowl off one step as opposed to having a run, and his competitive days were long behind him.

We often asked what was wrong with Dad, but we never got a straight answer. When our friends asked us what was wrong, we couldn't answer in a way that satisfied anybody's curiosity.

What is CMT?

Charcot-Marie-Tooth Disease is a genetic condition that damages peripheral nerves. These nerves are responsible for passing on commands from the brain to the muscles (motor nerves) and for passing information to the brain about sensations, such as pain, heat, cold, touch, importantly for balance – where your joints are in space (sensory nerves). When these are damaged, people are said to have a neuropathy.

Because of this nerve damage, people with CMT may find that some of their muscles have become slowly weaker over the years, particularly in their feet and hands. Some find that feeling becomes dull, or numb, in the same areas.

There are over 100 variations of CMT and people can be affected very differently, even those with the same type of CMT.

Ref www.cmt.org.uk

My diagnosis devastated Mum and Dad. It had been explained to me that CMT was hereditary. Mum and Dad never knew this. In fact, Dad had never even been given a proper diagnosis as to what caused his problems. He'd had a really poor experience at the hands of the medical profession in his attempts to establish what was wrong. He'd been called a malingerer and a time waster by Doctors who did not understand his symptoms and the issues he was presenting with. I can only imagine the anguish he must have felt when I received the diagnosis that also confirmed the root of his problems, and the fact that neither he or Mum had the knowledge and the explanations that could have saved me all the distress that I was going through – what decisions would they or I have made differently had we known? It's an imponderable question; we'll never know.

The reality is that they had no idea what Dad's problem was, and they decided to get married and have two children, myself and my younger brother Paul. Paul also has CMT.

The events of that period of my life would have consequences later on in terms of my mental health. I wasn't ready or able to accept it, but the rest of my life was about to start.

Start of Play

Mum and Dad were both born within a year of the 2nd World War ending, and were part of the baby boom generation of Birkenhead. They met whilst working on different stalls at Birkenhead market. They had a decent group of friends that also included Dad's younger brother, Kenny. They married in Birkenhead in 1968 and I came along two years later. Everton had just won the 1970 League Title and Dad wanted to call me Howard after Howard Kendall, but Mum won out, as she wanted a name that couldn't be shortened.

I was born at home, 58 Fieldside Road in Rock Ferry. Dad worked at the newly opened Vauxhall plant at Ellesmere Port, and then on the docks in Birkenhead. They'd grown up on Merseyside in the heyday of the music scene over the water in Liverpool. Mum was very much a lover of the Beatles and would often tell us, as we were growing up, of her times at The Cavern watching The Quarrymen, a band from Liverpool who were getting pretty decent reviews at the time. The Quarrymen, of course, went on to become the biggest band the world had ever seen and Mum was really proud of the fact that she saw them before the rest of the world had even heard of The Beatles.

Dad's nickname at the time was Jake. I assume this was derived from the fictional figure Jake the Peg, who had a dodgy leg. Indication from before I was born that Dad had a noticeable issue with his gait in his younger years. Until it got too much for him, he enjoyed football, cricket and the outdoors. He was a keen angler and was part of a club in Birkenhead that regularly took trips to Berriew in mid-Wales to fish on the River Severn. He probably looked forward to taking his eldest Son fishing with him. However, my memory of such trips was that Berriew was a long drive and that fishing bored the tits off me. It couldn't have been much fun for Dad having me with him. I was never one for sitting down quietly and enjoying the serenity of a quiet riverbank waiting for a trout to stir Dad into frenzied action by nibbling on a worm on the end of a hook. I seem to remember enjoying collecting wood for the fire on which to boil water for a brew in a Billy Can. But in all honesty that was about the highlight for me other than lunch now and again in a pub called the Talbot (I think).

Fortunately for Dad, Paul shared his love of nature much more than I did and they enjoyed going off fishing and bird watching together for years. We'd often spend time picking lead shot out of pheasants that had been acquired from somewhere and ended up in our garage. I can remember dad gutting plaice in the kitchen or handling massive crabs that were in buckets on the kitchen floor. Some of those things were monsters. The smells were disgusting and put me off eating fish for years.

I shared Dad's other interests, namely football and cricket. Dad was a massive Everton fan. He was always telling me how great Everton were and talking about his heroes in the '60s, Kendall, Ball and Harvey – The Holy Trinity. Alex Young, The Golden Vision, and of course the greatest of them all Dixie Dean. In 1966, Dad was a Panel Beater on Borough Road in Birkenhead, just up from Tranmere Rovers' ground. One day, Dixie Dean came in and asked for a repair to be done to his car. Dad said he'd do it but rather than receive payment in cash, could Dixie get him a ticket for the Cup final? Dixie duly obliged and Dad got to witness one of the great Cup finals of all time, with Everton coming from 2-0 down to beat Sheffield Wednesday 3-2. Dad loved the game but hated London and never went back again in his life.

By the time I was six or seventh, I was completely obsessed with football. Dad's brother Kenny did not have the problems that Dad had with his feet and legs. Like a lot of families on Merseyside, the football allegiances were different within the same family. Uncle Kenny was a Red and a season ticket holder at Anfield. Kenny could play, and I used to have hours of fun in gardens and on Woodchurch playing fields near my Grandad's house, playing football with Uncle Ken. It must have devastated Dad when I chose to support Liverpool at a really young age. Uncle Ken was made up, I'd get Liverpool kits for Christmas and Birthdays. Dad kept his counsel, at least to me anyway. Paul chose Everton and I'd like to think that Dad knew I'd see the light someday too. I did, eventually, but it was several years later. I am now well and truly over my flirtation with the dark side.

Dad's philosophy on life was that once you were married, your role as a man was to keep bread on the table. He is a bright fella and whilst I think he was capable of much more in a professional capacity, his working life was spent in a succession of blue-collar jobs on production lines and at Birkenhead Docks.

Mum was a lot more driven and had broader aspirations, if not always for herself, she certainly had them for Paul and I. Mum and Dad took the decision to move from Rock Ferry on the Wirral to a new housing development just outside Mold in North Wales. It was a 25-minute drive from where I was born, but I think their parents thought it was emigration. My parents flirted with the idea of emigrating to New Zealand on the old £10 ticket scheme, but Dad decided against it because upon further investigation, it seemed that his Kiwi employers would not be offering any overtime to boost his wages. It seems like madness now that they didn't take the opportunity but in Dad's mind, what was the point of emigrating if he couldn't earn the same money?

Paul was born in Chester in 1973. We had settled in a new build bungalow in Bryn-y-Baal on the outskirts of Mold. In our early years, Mum would work night shifts in the Cross Keys in Sychdyn to supplement Dad's income off the docks. Dad worked a lot of weekends and Paul and I would spend many weekends back in Birkenhead staying with Grandparents.

The highlight of these weekends for me would be visiting my Mum's parents, Harold (H) and Edith (known as Cissy) Newbury. H was the son of a Sailor in the Royal Navy from Portsmouth. He joined the Navy as a boy aged 14 and was educated at what is now the National Maritime Museum in Greenwich. He met Nanny Ciss when the ship he was serving on during WW2 docked in Birkenhead. Nanny Ciss's Mum ran a Sailor's Rest in Birkenhead and H went to stay there. They married on Boxing Day, 1943 and he promptly returned to sea and never came home until the end of the war in 1945.

H was the original Uncle Albert. Almost every story he told began with the line, "When I was in the Navy," or "Jawwing the War." He had me captivated from a very young age with his tales. He was one of this country's heroes – he was certainly mine. My Mum idolised him. Weekends with H and Nanny Ciss were brilliant. They would take us on the Ferry across to Liverpool and we'd go to Liverpool Museum. I loved it, just going back and forward on the ferry was great. I loved Birkenhead and Liverpool; it gave me a sense of where I was from. I wasn't Welsh, even though we lived there, I was from Birkenhead. Nan and Grandad lived in Tranmere, between the old St Catherine's Hospital and the Old Chester Road. A big set of steps linked their street to the Old Chester Road, the steps were known as the Monkey Steps and Grandad was still climbing them into his 90s. From their upstairs bedroom windows, you could see the river and Liverpool on the other side. Their house was built on a hillside and Nan would tell me that during the war, an air raid shelter was built into the hillside because the German Bombers would fly over Birkenhead and drop bombs on the docks on their way over to bomb Liverpool. Nan would tell us lots of stories about how the people of Birkenhead survived during those dark days and the community spirit that saw them through. As a young kid I lapped it all up. What a generation of people they were.

Weekends away at Grandparents continued until I was about 11, when I started playing regular football and cricket at weekends. By this time, Dad had been made redundant from the Docks and had started a new job at British Aerospace, now Airbus, at Broughton which was a bit closer to home at least. Mum had started a new job as a lecturer at Kelsterton College in Deeside. She taught students how to use punch card machines; these were the forerunners of PC's, which were to come in a few years later.

Throughout all this time, Dad's strength was deteriorating as a result of this disease that he had no knowledge about and didn't understand. It was getting worse and worse as he got older. Throughout all of this time he refused to accept that he needed help or support or that he was an individual with a disability. He epitomised the British stiff upper lip, we'll survive mentality – it hurts me to say it, but he lived with this attitude to the point of ignorance and ultimately selfishness; all because he believed it was the best way to deal with it. It became increasingly difficult to watch and we never knew how bad things would get. There was never any talk of the condition affecting me or Paul – it never entered our heads.

With both parents now working, we could afford some nice holidays. Mum and Dad took us to Malta, Italy and Yugoslavia. We'd previously been to Devon, where Mum dressed Paul and I in horrendous matching green and white striped cagoules. Funny how you remember traumatic fashion disasters.

All through my childhood, I never remember Dad's disability (my term, not his) causing us any problems. He was just our dad. He went out to work like anyone else did.

I never remember Dad saying he couldn't do something because of his legs when I was a kid. Wherever I played football or cricket, he was there watching. But we never seemed to go for many days out anywhere. We never went to the cinema with our parents. Dad never took me to football matches, but that might have been because in my younger years I was a Red; can't blame him for not wanting to take me there. But then he never took me to cricket matches either. I remember him and Mum buying a pair of tickets to go and watch England v West Indies; it must have been around 1980 at Old Trafford. They got there and took their seats next to a West Indian couple. The heavens opened and they never saw a ball being bowled and sat next to the two West Indians who were getting smashed on rum. They vowed never to go again.

All that mattered to me as a kid was playing football and playing cricket. I did other usual things that kids did, like going to Cubs and Scouts, but once they got in the way of football or cricket practice, they were dropped. I didn't want distractions.

My first real memory of cricket was the 1981 Ashes Series. I remember sitting and watching it on the TV absolutely spellbound by Botham and Willis and the context in which Botham in particular was performing. He'd been the captain, suffered a bad run of form, clashed with the administrators and been sacked. Then all of a sudden, here he was, performing like the absolute legend we all knew he was. I was hooked on cricket after that. I wanted to play like Botham or his mate Viv Richards, smashing 4's and 6's and bowling as fast as I could.

Every summer was spent in the cricket nets at school, all day every day of the school holidays. There was a group of us: me, Andy Darlington, Ian Allen, John Hill, Cooper and Mushy, and often we were joined by Tim Willesdon, a giant of a lad who bowled quick and got good bounce because of his height. These were the days before helmets were easily available and Tim certainly kept you on your toes. We all played for the local village club, from Under-11's right through to senior cricket.

Dad taught me a lesson really early on in life that stuck with me. I never had any pads or gloves of my own so if I wanted to practice, I would borrow kit from the local cricket club. Our manager lived down the road and he held the club kitbag. The first time that I borrowed a pair of pads, I returned home to drop my bat off before setting off to return the pads. Dad called me back and suggested that I might want to put some whitener on the pads before returning them. As a stroppy 12-year-old, I couldn't see the point in doing that. I hadn't dirtied the pads, they were dirty when I collected them. Wisely, Dad said if I returned them in a better condition than I collected them, it would be unlikely that I'd ever be refused when I requested to borrow kit again in the future. Sure enough, over the years, I never was. I was one of those cricketers who took pride in his kit and looking the part. All the gear, no idea. That was me.

We never received what I now understand as proper coaching. As we got a bit older and were invited to net with the Club first XI there'd be the odd word of advice here and there but never proper coaching. I made my debut for the first-XI when I was 12 or 13. They were obviously short, and I was keen as mustard and was never going to turn down the opportunity.

It wasn't the experience that I'd hoped it would be. Our wicketkeeper at the time was what I'd now describe as an arsehole. I remember misfielding at third-man and he went absolutely off his head. Bawling at me from behind the stumps, then clapping sarcastically when I stopped the next one. It was a horrible experience. Week after week I'd turn out to make the numbers up and this prick would use me as the butt of his humour. I was too shy and lacking in the confidence to have a go back. Week by week, my confidence and enjoyment of Saturday league cricket drained away; but I still turned up because I loved the game.

They'd noticed that I had a particular style when I ran. I wasn't aware of this but it looked as if my lower legs were going to fly off at the knee when I sprinted. I'd be chasing after the ball and our wicketkeeper would be shouting, "Mind those legs don't fall off Ian." None of this did anything for my confidence at all.

Further reference to there being particular anomalies with my gait came when me and a couple of mates would walk down from our village to the nearest town after playing football on a Saturday morning. They noticed that my feet slapped on the ground a lot when I walked. I never noticed it but they pointed it out and would often giggle behind my back about it. Again, this did nothing for my confidence and I was beginning to get a complex about my feet and legs. I'd be looking in football magazines and seeing the well-developed quads and calves of footballers, and wondering why, given all the exercise I was doing, did my legs not look like that. Obviously, now it was a ridiculous comparison to make but I was definitely starting to get a bit of a complex.

There'd always be somebody taking the piss at one level or another about my skinny legs, bandy legged walk or funny running style. It was strange to me because I couldn't see it. I was competing well at football. I was a half-decent bat and as fast as anyone bowling in my age group, and I was a decent cross-country or middle-distance runner. I was holding my own so there was no reason to think that I was suffering with any of the issues that Dad had.

During the winter, football took priority for me. Living in Wales, Rugby was the main winter sport in school. I just couldn't get into it. It was always about football for me and Liverpool were the most successful side around at the time. Our house backed onto our junior school field so it was easy to jump over the fence and go and have a kick about. Loads of us used to turn up, including those that didn't go to our village school because they went to local Catholic schools. It was a great way to meet other kids in the area. That's one of the beauties of sport; it just brings people together. Half the time we didn't know everybody's name, and shortened names or nicknames were developed. There was Suey, Miff, Haggis, Bod, Beanhead, Mill, Datty, Ching, Oily, Tommo, Irish, Chewy and Tigger to name a few… oh and mine, Tashy.

As I mentioned earlier, during the impressionable and formative years of my life that included my introduction to football, I was in awe of my Uncle Ken. He was the guy that sparked my passion for football and I wanted to be like him, and not like my dad who couldn't run. Harsh, but true. Uncle Ken supported Liverpool and they'd won the European Cup, and he bought me the latest Liverpool shirt with their new shirt sponsor, Hitachi, emblazoned across the front. Playing football with lads who were either older than me or from different schools and who didn't know my name, made them refer to me as Hitachi, as it was written on my shirt. This got shortened to Tachi, then to Tashy or Tash. It's stayed with me for life. I've never been able to shake it off, not that I've tried that hard, to be honest.

It now gets used by my wife and kids. If we get lost when out in the car, one of them will pipe up, "Oh here we are again, on Tashies Tours." If I get pissed off, it will be, "Oh no, a Tashy Tantrum." If they need a lift, it's "Tashy Taxi's". If I buy myself a new shirt, it's a "Tashy Treat". The list is endless and often tiresome. Nothing quite like family to keep your feet on the ground.

But the one that causes most amusement amongst my oldest mates is "Turncoat Tashy". Nowadays, Liverpool supporters get lots of stick about being armchair fans who never go to the game. Well, I can confirm that it was forever so. As well as me, there were loads of kids in our school who said that they supported Liverpool. I can't remember any that actually went to the game, myself included. Dad wouldn't take me. Uncle Kenny had a season ticket with his mates and nobody from school went. Between the ages of seven and 13, I went to four games at Anfield. I was getting disillusioned with saying I supported a team, but never actually going to watch them. Of the group I knocked around with in school, nobody supported Liverpool; they were all Everton.

Since Dad had stopped working on the Docks, we were seeing less of Uncle Kenny. On a Saturday or midweek, my mates from school would get on the bus at the Griffin and go and watch Everton. It was 1983. Liverpool were getting sold by the media as being the best team in history. Everton, on the other hand, had just appointed Howard Kendall as manager and were in deep shit at the bottom end of the table. Liverpool (the greatest team in the world, remember?) were playing Burnley in the Semi-final 2nd leg of the Milk Cup at Turf Moor. Liverpool had won the first leg 3-0 against the lower league opposition. That night, Burnley were magnificent. They played so well and came away with a 1-0 win. I was really disillusioned with Liverpool and felt no real connection to them any longer. It was all very well, saying how great they were, but there was nobody in my life outside of Uncle Kenny, whom I didn't see that much of anymore, and Mum's brother, my Uncle Brian, who didn't go that often, to connect me to the club. Yet, Everton had my dad, my brother and a load of my mates, and they went to watch their club. Everton were really poor too at that time.

Decision made. I was turning.

The following day, I gathered up all my Liverpool FC memorabilia and took it down to my mate Chingy. He was a Red, and his dad, Brian, was a blue. Brian was delighted with my decision but Chingy hasn't stopped taking the piss out of me since. It even got mentioned at my wedding some years later, as Ching delivered the best man's speech.

The following year I got my first Season Ticket on the Gwladys Street and I've never looked back. I was lucky. The Everton team of the mid-eighties became the best team the club has ever had. That team gave me some of the best times of my childhood, the football that they played was amazing and the crack that I had with my mates going to watch them was also great. Evertonians still talk in reverence about that team now and some of the games we saw in the 1984/85 season. We were turning up at Goodison, wondering not whether we were going to win, but by how many. The highlight was the Bayern Munich game; 50,000 crammed into Goodison under the floodlights on a late April evening. The place was bouncing in the way only Goodison can. But there were other games too that I'll never forget: beating Man United 5-0, beating Sunderland 4-1 when Andy Gray scored two of the best diving headers you'll ever see and Paul Bracewell played "that" pass cross-field to Trevor Steven to cut inside and score. I was there for all of it and it was brilliant. I could talk forever about that period in Everton's history to my son, as my dad talked to me about the Holy Trinity of Kendall, Ball and Harvey and the Golden Vision, Alex Young.

That's the thing about football; taking my son, Conor, to his first game felt a little bit like passing the baton on to the next generation. He knows how much I love Everton, and Goodison in particular, and he'll remember the times we shared there for a long time after I've passed on and will hopefully pass the baton on to his kids. Now that I'm a father, I can definitely appreciate my dad's patience and tolerance when I was spouting off about Liverpool when I was seven and eight. I wouldn't have stood for any of that off Conor. There's a shed in the garden for a reason.

Of course, Everton's destiny was curtailed by events at Heysel in the summer of 1985. The ban on English teams entering European competitions was devastating for Everton. We were comfortably the best team in Europe at the time and we were looking forward to playing in the following season's European Cup, but it wasn't to be.

All I wanted to do as a kid was play either cricket or football for a living. By the age of 12, I realised I was probably never going to do either. I was never going to cut it as a footballer, and with the benefit of hindsight, I was much more enthusiastic than talented as a cricketer. Loving the game wasn't going to translate into a career. Or at least not in the way that I expected, but more of that later.

Grandad H had the Navy running through his blood. A distant cousin of mine, Stuart Baird was also in the Navy. In 1982, Argentina invaded the Falkland Islands and Stuart was a weapons engineer on HMS Exeter. Exeter was despatched to the South Atlantic as part of the Task Force sent by Mrs Thatcher to recover the Islands and return them to British Sovereignty. I was 12 and I followed proceedings intently. The Falklands War ended in the June and I remember watching TV as HMS Hermes and HMS Invincible returned back to the UK.

Soon enough, HMS Exeter returned, and a family party was held at H's house to welcome Stuart safely back home. I sat on the freezer in Grandad's kitchen, as Stuart told us all about his experiences. I must have been like a starry-eyed kid. All I knew was that I wanted some of this life. Grandad had talked about it but Stuart was out there living it, and I decided that night, that is what I wanted to do.

It was kind of an epiphany. I never once waivered from the ambition to join the Navy. School became a bit procedural; something I had to endure before I could join up. Mum tried to steer me down the route of becoming an Officer or an Artificer and we went to a number of different recruitment events. The Careers advisor in school was a lady called Mrs Mitchelhill and she was really supportive. I just wanted the fastest career route to get to sea and start living the life.

Dad had his set ideas. I never felt completely sure that he wanted me to join the Navy. I sensed he would be much happier if I'd gotten an apprenticeship at Airbus. He would often tell me that a good skill and an apprenticeship will give you a job for life. There may have been some truth in that but all I saw was a guy chained to a mortgage and a 9 to 5 job. I was 15 by now and there was plenty of time for all of that.

My 'O' Level exams in June 1986 were a bit of a joke. I had little interest; I knew what I was going to be doing and I didn't need exams. Besides, the 1986 World Cup was going on in Mexico right at the time my exams were taking place. With the time difference, it meant that I was up until all hours of the morning, most nights watching the football. The England team was full of Everton players at the time and Gary Lineker was the tournament's top scorer before he returned to England and left Everton to join Barcelona. I remember watching Peter Reid chasing Maradona as he went through to score his second goal for Argentina to put England out of the tournament, in the match mostly remembered for the Hand of God incident. I left school having achieved one 'O' Level. I was a bit embarrassed but not surprised, I really didn't put the work in. I wasn't particularly pleased at having achieved O Level English either, because I felt that I should have been able to gain a qualification in a language I'd been speaking since I could talk. I must also confess that I used lyrics from a Madness song in one of the essays that I wrote in my English Language exam. Did the job though. Thanks Suggs.

I was offered a place in the Royal Navy when I was 16, just as I was finishing high school. However, I couldn't actually start until I was 16 and a half. I had six months to kill before I could join up. Dad got me an interview at Airbus for the YTS scheme. £32 per fortnight for training and learning different skills needed on the production line at Airbus. I started with a mate of mine from school, Mike Whitley. It was a late August morning, and we were standing waiting for a bus to get us down to the factory for a 7:30 am start. It already felt like hell and it didn't get any better when Mum took £10 for keep, out of my first pay packet.

Six months of my life that I will never get back, but at least it confirmed that a life on a production line was not for me. Why Dad could not see this, is beyond me. Paul and I were never encouraged to study hard or to go to university. To be fair, it wouldn't have mattered to me because my mind was made up about joining the Navy, but Dad just didn't seem to have any hopes for Paul or me to aspire to have a better life than he'd made for himself; or if he did, he never showed it.

Paul took the Airbus route. He was really talented with his hands and could turn his hand to most things. He secured an apprenticeship to become a French Polisher and ended up working on some of the Queen's Flight. He was the first apprentice French polisher that the company had taken on, and some of the restorations he delivered were just out of this world; so talented. Paul worked on the plane that flew Princess Diana's body back from Paris after she had died, and on the private jets of many a successful businessman.

I finished at Airbus before Christmas. It felt like a huge relief. On Christmas Day 1986, there was a program on the TV called *Rock Around the Rock*. Basically, it was different pop music acts performing on the flight deck of HMS Ark Royal in Gibraltar. I sat and watched and wondered, where I would be in 12 months' time. I desperately wanted to join Ark Royal. It was the most famous ship in the fleet and also the Navy's flagship. I wanted to be part of that.

All at Sea

Christmas came and went, and on the morning of 26th January 1987, Mum dropped me off at Buckley station to catch the train down to Plymouth, where I would be met and taken to the Navy's New Entry Training Establishment, HMS Raleigh in Torpoint, just over the river from Plymouth.

I'd said goodbye to Mum, not really knowing when I was going to see her again. An adventure that would take me all over the world and give me so many experiences and shape me as bloke, was about to start. I didn't think too much about anyone other than Grandad H. He would be so proud of me. I just needed to get through the basic training, and get to sea, and then I'd be just like him.

Some of the lads that I went to school with, also joined the military. Some joined the Army, a couple joined the RAF, and my good friend Matt joined the Royal Marines. I was the only one who joined the Navy. This of course led to more mickey taking, "don't drop the soap in the shower" and "ooh hello sailor" became regular jibes. I'd never heard of the Navy's reputation for being popular with men of a certain sexual orientation; it was news to me. I was also told that a lad from the school in the village next to ours was also joining up on the same day as me. His cousin went to my school and she delighted in telling me how her 'really hard' cousin was going to beat me up when he met me because apparently I was a bit of a "puff".

So, it was with all this in mind that I journeyed with excitement and an equal measure of trepidation into the unknown, really not sure about what I had let myself in for. I needn't have worried. The group I trained with were a great set of lads, a mix of all ages and backgrounds. Me and the 'really hard' lad from the next village got on really well. It's funny how reputations feel huge when you are so young but when you are put in an environment such as military basic training, everything becomes a bit of a leveller. Growing up in semi-rural North Wales is a small world. At 16, you think you know it all, but then meeting lads from the inner cities, you realise you know nothing. Me and the local hard nut knew nothing – green as grass as I began to realise. Being around these guys, I began to realise how fortunate my upbringing was, but I also learned what the rest of the country thought of anyone with a scouse accent.

Basic training is designed to bring about a couple of outcomes. First and foremost, the aim is to train and develop recruits to a level where they are able to join the fleet, the regular Navy, and contribute effectively. The second aim complements the first, in that they aim to make sure that only the recruits with the right character and resilience get through. You could be the fittest, the strongest or the most academically capable, but if you crumble when under pressure, then the military probably isn't the life for you. It was a real shock to the system for me, but then it's designed to be.

I was good at most of the academic side of training, but I started to struggle with some of the physical stuff. Unsurprisingly, the Navy wanted you to complete their basic swimming test. This consisted of two lengths of the pool, wearing overalls and boots, then three minutes treading water without touching the bottom or the sides. Then you had to get out of the pool and climb up to the diving board (10 meter, I think) and jump in and swim to the side.

I could do the "swim and the jump off the board", but I could not tread water to save my life (no pun intended but that was the object of the exercise should you end up in the sea at any point in the future). I ended up having to retake the test time and again, I just couldn't get it right.

The assault course at Raleigh was something that I was really looking forward to and we got our first exposure to it in Week 2, I think. Again, this was to be completed in overalls and boots. It's a misconception to think that the idea is to get around it as quickly as possible. In the military, there's no point in achieving the objective on your own if the rest of your team are left behind. Halfway around, I jumped into a lake that we had to cross and get out on the other side. As I landed in the water my right ankle twisted really badly, it was agony. So many thoughts went through my head; *Am I going to get back classed? Will they kick me out? Is it bad? Can I run it off?*

I clambered out of the lake, and I must have looked like I'd been shot in the leg. I struggled to run but I was close to completing the course and was desperate to do so. This gave the sadistic PTIs license to hurl a dog's abuse at me. "What's up with you? Is it too difficult for you, do you want to go home, do you want to see your Mummy?" All interspersed with the finest Anglo-Saxon. They made quite sure that you felt like an unimportant piece of shit, and they enquired why they were wasting their time with such a waste of space. I crawled under the crawling nets and then through a drainpipe half-filled with water to get to the other side where the finish line was. To finish, you had to climb over a decent-sized wall where one of the lads was sitting and was heaving everybody over the wall.

Eventually, I got the ankle checked out. No x-rays, or anything as sophisticated as that. It was decided that it wasn't broken; at worst it was a cracked bone and ligament damage, or at best a bad sprain. If it's still sore in a week, come back. A bit of tubigrip and a couple of painkillers later, I was back with the lads. The ankle hampered me with everything, not just the fitness side of things; it was so painful and I still needed to pass this bloody swimming test.

The weeks went by and whilst the swelling went down, it was obvious that the ankle was really weak and very easy to turn again, and so painful. I'd managed to keep my head down and got on with things as best I could. I recall that my happiest moments during basic training were cleaning the Heads (that's toilets in Navy Speak). I'd volunteer for it if I could because it gave me the opportunity to get my headphones on and listen to some music and just escape for a little while. I remember that my toilet scrubbing soundtrack was the Housemartin's "London 0 Hull 4" album. Every time I hear the song "Happy Hour", it takes me back to scrubbing toilets at HMS Raleigh. Funny how little things like that become essential treats during tough times.

There was nothing that the instructors wouldn't take the piss out of.

"Is that a photo of your girlfriend, have you got any nude photos of her?"

"No, Chief," would come the reply.

"Well would you like me to give you some?" the Chief would respond. It was all about provoking a reaction. They would wake you up at three in the morning and have you doing drill exercises in the yard outside the accommodation block. Then you'd go back to bed only for the alarm to wake you at 6 to begin the next day's activities.

With one week to go before I was due to pass out of basic training, I still hadn't passed the swimming test. It was starting to look a bit touch-and-go as to whether I was going to do it or not. Finally, I cracked it. The best way to stay afloat in the water is with minimal movement and to tip your head so far back that you are almost looking behind you. The weight of your head and the buoyancy of the water automatically make your legs raise, and there you are, floating. Three minutes? I could stay there for three hours now that I'd figured it out.

So, the feeling of achievement on the day of my passing out parade was huge. Mum, Dad, Paul, Uncle Kenny and Aunty Pat all came down to watch. The saying that "nothing worth having ever comes easy", sums up the whole experience. Confidence is a funny thing. You can't turn it on or off. You think some people have it in abundance but often they don't. I was really overawed when I first joined up. I was too easily pushed around and easily influenced. Like many kids at that age, all I wanted was to fit in and be liked by the people I grew up with at home. Then there were all these blokes who I joined up with, all with different backgrounds and different stories, and maybe some of the same anxieties, but we were all in this together, I was the youngest, the eldest was 32. I realised that I was as good as any of them. One night, whilst waiting to make a short phone call home, I saw the guy from the next village to me, the one who was supposedly dead hard and was going to beat me up. He was crying his eyes out to his Mum because things were tough, and he was homesick. I learnt that hardness and toughness present themselves in different ways, and that mental toughness and resilience are more valuable commodities to me than physical brawn. Basic training sorts you out. The hard nuts could not make it through unless they had a character to go with it. Lads failed training because they lacked the discipline and character to go with their strength. The Navy wanted people that they could rely on in battle, not people with huge egos and no substance.

You can't blag this sort of stuff because eventually you get found out. The team comes first, and the team is only as strong as its weakest member. The weakest member might not be the person you first think it is. By getting close to people and seeing them at their lowest, there comes honesty, and trust, developed through the sharing or the exposure of vulnerability. Basic training does this in a controlled way – everybody receives a crew cut on the first day. Therefore, anyone who turns up looking super cool with great hair is immediately reduced to being one of the group, not someone who stands out. The military looks for people to stand out in a different way. You might think you're a big fish where you grew up but once you enter a military training, establishment you have it all to prove. Respect is earned and not given out freely.

Everybody has a moment in the spotlight where they are ripped to pieces by the training staff. I wouldn't go as far as to say that they are trying to break you, but it is certainly about testing your character, and seeing how you handle your emotions when you're tired, pissed off and someone is two inches from your nose, telling you how useless you are.

Once your vulnerability is acknowledged, I would argue that far from being in a position of weakness, you are actually in a position of the greatest strength. Having the humility and self-awareness to acknowledge an area of your own vulnerability is the gateway to growth in that area and further development, and whatever creativity is needed to close the gap on where you are and where you want to be. When you can do this, I would say that you are comfortable with who you are and the skin that you're in.

Better this than living your life running away from a fear of failure or weakness. It took me years and a lot of self-reflection to learn this lesson and live by it, but Basic Training with the Navy certainly put me on the right track.

After completing my trade training as a Radar Operator at HMS Dryad in Hampshire, it was time to go to sea. We were all asked to submit requests for what type of ship we wished to join. I requested an Aircraft Carrier. I desperately wanted Ark Royal or a Type 42 destroyer. Our course leader read out a list of the ships that were available to us, and sure enough, Ark Royal was one of them. It turned out that one of the other guys sat in the room with us also wanted Ark Royal because his brother was already serving onboard. This presented me with a bit of a moral dilemma. Should I defer to him and let him serve at sea with his brother, thereby forgoing my opportunity to realise an ambition?

No Chance.

We both placed our ID cards in a hat. The Petty Officer in charge gave the hat a shake and closed his eyes. I don't know why, but I knew he would pull my ID card out of the hat. It was never in doubt; I wanted it so much. Sure enough, he said, "Congratulations Martin, you're joining Ark Royal." I was delighted. I think the other guy got HMS Liverpool. I went home on leave and got my joining instructions through the post. I joined HMS Ark Royal in August 1987.

A Life on The Ocean Waves – HMS ARK ROYAL

The next two years were amazing. A lot of hard work, but a hell of a lot more good times. Every morning you'd see a face you'd not seen before at breakfast; Ark Royal was like a floating village. There was a shop, a laundry, a post office and a bank/travel exchange. There was a dentist and a mini hospital with doctors and nurses. The laundry was the biggest surprise to me. I'd heard of the phrase "Chinese Laundry" but I'd never seen one. Ark Royal had its very own, staffed by about a dozen Hong Kong locals, only a couple of which could speak English. They worked night and day, making sure our uniforms were clean, pressed and ready for the next day. They would do uniform alterations and sow badges onto kit as you got promoted. They were also the biggest gamblers I've ever seen.

They'd bet on two cockroaches running across the floor.

We went to some amazing places in the two years that I was onboard. My first proper run ashore was Hamburg, a real eye-opener to 17-year-old me. Never seen anything like it. As the youngest onboard, the others made it their mission to get me sold to a variety of young ladies down the Reeperbahn – I resisted; honestly. What a place! The following year we went on deployment for six months to the Far East and Australia. This is what I joined the Navy for.

We got to Singapore via a short stop in Malta, and down the Suez Canal where some of us went to Cairo and to see the Sphinx and the Pyramids. The Suez and the Red Sea were the hottest temperatures I had ever experienced. Sailing across the Indian Ocean on Ark Royal were some of the happiest times of my life. I would always volunteer to sit in a contraption called the Bosun's Chair. Essentially it is nothing more than a plank of wood that forms a seat which is then lowered down the outboard side of the ship by ropes to enable a sailor to paint or repair damage to the ship's hull. I loved it and would spend as many hours as I could hanging off the side of Ark Royal in just a pair of tropical shorts, catching the sun and painting. These were times when I had to pinch myself; I was literally loving life.

The other strong memory that I have is of coming off the middle watch at 4 in the morning and going to the galley to get freshly made bread rolls and sausages, with lashings of brown sauce. The smell of the freshly made bread was amazing and these were the best sausage baps I would ever eat – I'd go up to one of the berthing bays where the RIBs (Rigid Inflatable Boats) were housed, and sit and watch the sunrise before going to bed to catch up on some sleep.

Speaking of the berthing bays, Ark Royal had a number of these different outboard spaces along both Port and Starboard sides of the ship. They were used for different purposes such as launching the RIB's or lowering a boarding ladder etc. Whilst I was loving life at sea, there were times when life got a little bit boring for some. *Welcome On Board the Phantom Shitter!*

Each morning, for about 10 days or so, someone would report having found a freshly laid turd in one of the berthing bays. It became one of the great nautical mysteries. "They seek him here, they seek him there, they seek the shitter everywhere." Nobody knew the identity of the Phantom Shitter but he was responsible for raising the spirits of many with his undercover dirty antics. Then, as quickly as the deposits began, they ended. We never identified him.

One of the age-old rituals that has existed in the Royal Navy for years is to pay homage to King Neptune whenever a ship sails over the equator. Ark Royal was no different and the flight deck was used to provide the setting for sailors to pay their respects.

A large swimming pool was erected and filled initially with water. The pool was big enough for a small stage to be placed inside it, which would form King Neptune's throne. Neptune was played by a gnarly old Chief Petty Officer with a long grey beard and a crown, wearing nothing more than a loincloth. Neptune took his seat on the throne and had two hairy-arsed sailors dressed as mermaids alongside him. Members of the ships company who had not sailed over the equator before were called forward in alphabetical order to pay homage to King Neptune. At this point, I really wished my surname was Aardvark because the longer this ceremony went on, the more disgusting the contents of the pool became.

As your name was called, you had to climb up the ladder and enter the pool and make your way through the filth to the feet of King Neptune. You then had to sit on a chair and what looked like a sweet was placed on your tongue. Don't think this was pleasant; the sweet was a pear drop sized piece of soap. Neptune then tipped your chair backwards and you were submerged in the filthy water before you exited the court of King Neptune. Quite the experience. Those with surnames beginning with W, Y and Z had it worse than most as they were submerged in a mixture of urine from the sailors who had passed through previously, leftovers and slops from the galley and anything else that the ship's company felt would be appropriate to add to the mix. It was grim.

After Singapore, we went to Hong Kong where I injured my elbow on a monumental night out. We were heading to a club called Joe Banana's, which was an old sailor's haunt recommended to us by some salts in the old China Fleet Club. I ran and jumped on one of the lad's back as he was running down the street. One of the other guys decided it would be fun to push me over the top. I put my arms out to break my fall and I immediately knew I'd done something to my arm. Nevertheless, we carried on into the night making the most of what Hong Kong had to offer.

Next morning it wasn't just my head that hurt. I went to see the Doc who sent me over to Kowloon and the British Army hospital there for an x-ray. Turned out, I'd chipped the bone in my elbow. So, with my arm in a sling, I returned back to the ship. I could no longer climb the ladders on the masts to paint or hang off the ship's side on a Bosun's Chair to do any painting there either – bit of a shame if I'm honest, because I enjoyed the solitude; the sun and the wind in my hair as the biggest ship in the fleet crossed the Indian Ocean. Instead I was sent to work in the cash office.

We left Hong Kong and went to Subic Bay in the Philippines. What a place that was. It was like the wild west, anything went. Subic Bay was the name of a big American naval base in a place called Olongapo City. The base was huge, and was guarded by a platoon of US Marines. We couldn't wait to get ashore and sample the delights of Olongapo. This place was a deviant's playground, a sailor's delight. There were loads of US Navy females around who were delighted to meet us British sailors, and there were bars with all the local girls (well most of them were girls, I think). We were warned about "chicks with dicks". I just couldn't believe it was even a thing, there was nothing like that in Mynydd Isa. Sure enough, after one night ashore the messdecks were full of stories of sailors having the shock of their lives when things got lively the night before. We were sharing tips on how to recognise them, large Adam's apples, large hairy hands; I'm not sure that any of us could have picked one out before it was too late. It didn't help that they were all stunning. Olongapo City was wild, like nowhere I had ever been before or since. You could walk into a bar and find your mate from the mess enjoying oral sex off some girl (?) under the table whilst enjoying a beer. There were no rules here – anything went. .

One night, I ventured out with one of the lads for a beer in one of the local bars. One beer turned into several and we decided to make our way back to the ship via what passed as the high street. We entered a local craft shop. There was an old boy sitting on his haunches, carving wooden gifts, presumably to sell to visiting sailors. Some of his work was exquisite, and clearly he'd spent hours making this stuff. Unfortunately for him, I found a set of nuncheckers – two wooden bars attached together by a rope that is used in martial arts. "Woah, these are brilliant," I explained to my mate. A cousin of my mate Ching back home used to use these and it was really impressive, so I thought it was a good idea to show my pal how these things worked. Bad move. Nuncheckers belong in the hands of trained experts and not pissed up sailors. I sent them flying across the store, taking out a whole row of this fella's hand-crafted gifts. We ran out of the store and were off down the street in a flash. We turned round and there was the shop owner, chasing after us in just his loincloth, as fast as he could, waving a machete. I've never been so glad to see a dockyard gate and a US Marine with a rifle.

After we left ports and some mornings whilst we were in ports for a week or so, I noticed that there was a queue outside the sick bay. I wondered what it was because they never advertised these clinics; so what were they for? "Oh, that's the queue for the dirty dick doctor," I was reliably informed. Sailors being sailors lived by the old motto of any port in a storm but unfortunately some of the ports that were visited were not as clean as one might have hoped for, The Dirty Dick Dr was never short of patients and it was a real rogues' gallery that lined up outside the clinic. If you saw one of your mates in the queue, it provided entertainment for ages.

"Where's Smudge?"

"Oh he's gone to see the Dirty Dick Dr; went with a local girl the other night and now his dick looks like a cauliflower."

We left the Philippines and headed off to Australia. This was the stuff of dreams for me and the exact reason why I joined up. Our first port of call was Brisbane. After a few days there, we went down to Sydney where we berthed at the Ocean Liner terminal in Circular Quay. I remember heading up to the flight deck and there was Sydney Opera House over to the right and the Harbour Bridge over to the left. I had to pinch myself; *what on earth was I doing here?*

Some of the lads had met girls in Brisbane who were on the quayside when we got to Sydney. The rest of us headed up to King's Cross and George Street to sample the local hospitality.

You might not believe this, but the ship ran a scheme called dial-a-sailor. The idea being that locals could call into the ship and offer to show the crew around Sydney, take them for dinner etc. This was a Community Engagement program that I could align with. By now, I was 18 years old and this seemed just the type of scheme that I needed to get closer to.

Fortunately, I knew the guy who worked on the ship's telephone exchange; so when the calls came in, I was able make sure he had my name down as someone who might be interested in being wined and dined by a local. There were caveats of course; I was looking for a young female and not an ex-sailor and his wife who'd emigrated to Sydney after the war. There were loads of calls that came in, mostly from ex-sailors or the widows of former sailors who just wanted to reminisce about the Navy. Occasionally, however, we struck gold and a pair of female students would call in, wanting to show a couple of sailors around the city. I was on hand on such occasions to represent Queen and Country and allow the young ladies to fulfil their request. It really wasn't a hardship. Whilst no medals were given out for this type of service, I can tell you that I went above and beyond, often alone, but sometimes with a wingman.

Another unexpected experience was when Australian Vogue came on board and wanted to shoot some shots including British sailors. I was one of the youngest onboard at the time and my presence was requested in uniform on the flight deck. Before I knew it, myself and several others were vogueing for the cameras and marching up and down the flight deck, whilst a photographer took loads of shots. We made a feature in Australian Vogue but I don't think any of us got asked back for more.

We were in Sydney for two weeks for the celebration of Australia's Bi-Centenary. It was 200 years since Captain Cook had first stepped foot in Oz. The celebrations were amazing, there was a big fleet review in Sydney Harbour, ships from all over the world had come to join in the party. Ark Royal was the centre of attention and when walking around the streets of Sydney in our uniforms, I, for one, felt so proud. The attention that we attracted was unbelievable; I'd never experienced anything like it. The firework display was just like you see at Sydney

Harbour on New Year's Eve, really spectacular, and we partied well into the night on most nights.

Over the two weeks I got to see most of the attractions, the Bridge, Bondi and Manley Beaches, Darling Harbour, the SCG, Centre Point Tower and of course the Opera House. I didn't cover myself in glory at the Opera House. A group of us arrived there after a lively afternoon drinking session around the city. Elton John was playing that evening and we convinced ourselves that Elton would be only too pleased to allow a load of British sailors into the audience to watch his show. We staggered up the steps to the entrance where we found that security didn't quite share our view of how delighted Elton would be to see us. We argued and argued and must have stretched the patience of the security staff until we realised the futility of our attempts to gain entry, and we sloped away dejectedly. By this time, the effects of the afternoon's excesses were beginning to take their toll on me. We got somewhere near the bottom of the steps leading up to the Opera House, and with the spectacular backdrop of the Harbour, the Bridge, the Opera House and our ship behind me, I delivered a technicolour yawn all over the steps. Not my proudest moment but I at least avoided ruining my uniform.

We left Sydney, probably in need of a few days at sea, to recover from what had been an amazing two weeks. We set sail for Melbourne and arrived in Port Phillip Bay to learn that the dock yard workers in Melbourne had gone on strike. They were refusing to let Ark Royal into port because they believed we had nuclear weapons on board. Our government's policy is always to neither confirm nor deny, and so a stand-off ensued. In the end it was decided that we would skip the visit to Melbourne and set sail for Fremantle on the west coast.

I have to admit that the voyage from Melbourne around to Fremantle was the toughest that I had experienced in terms of rough seas. The passage around and underneath Australia is called the Great Australian Bight; you've got three oceans coming together, the Pacific from the east, the Southern Ocean from, you've guessed it, the south and the Indian Ocean from the west. It tossed the Ark Royal around like a cork in a bath tub. I was so rough.

One of the most enjoyable things about being at sea was when the ship was rolling a little bit and you were nodding off to sleep, it was a great way to relax. That stretch of water, however, was not quite so relaxing; our bunks had straps on them to make sure you didn't roll out, and I was certainly glad of them then. The only other time that I was close to being seasick was when we were sailing through the Bay of Biscay and the area known as the South West Approaches, where the Atlantic meets the English Channel – it can get a bit ropey there too.

Fremantle was great. A huge dockyard which serviced the city of Perth. Freo, as the locals called it, seemed like a bit of a step back in time. A lot of, what I'd describe as, 1920s architecture, but it was charming; a really nice place. I remember, in particular, spending a lot of time on the beach there, and there was a McDonald's right on the beach too which was a favourite with the lads. Perth was good too. Very modern with some great restaurants, but most of our down time was spent in bars or on Cottesloe Beach, which was one of the best beaches I'd been to at that point in my life.

It was in Fremantle that one of my mates Paul, or Spongey (Spun-gee) as he was known after getting pissed one night and soaking his bunk on board, advised me that he was going to jump ship. He'd met a girl in Brisbane. She followed him around Australia, everywhere the Ark Royal tied up, Raelene was on the quayside waiting for him. This was all very nice but jumping ship and risking your liberty if you get caught is a whole different ball game. Spongey asked if I'd empty his locker and put all of his belongings in a bin bag. He then wanted me to take the bag ashore as if I was taking a bag of rubbish off the ship to put in one of the quayside skips.

Now, Raelene was a lovely girl, really pretty and obviously into him given the miles she'd covered just to see him, and if ever the phrase "punching above his weight" applied to anyone, it applied to Spongey. I could certainly see the appeal of jumping ship in Australia and living happily ever after with Raelene. Once you take your head out of the clouds though, it's impossible to believe you could ever get away with it. But he was insistent that this was what he wanted to do. I was his best mate on board and so I felt duty-bound to help him, regardless of what would happen to me if I was caught assisting someone to abscond.

So the night before we were due to sail from Fremantle up to Bombay, I emptied Spongey's locker and placed all of his belongings in a bin bag. On my way ashore to meet him for a beer, I left the bag behind a skip on the jetty. My heart was pumping as I left the ship. If that bag had split whilst I was walking down the gangway, I'd be in deep shit. I left the dockyard and met Spongey and Raelene in town. "Job done," I told him. We enjoyed a few beers, I wished him well and returned to the ship. I thought he had some balls to be doing what he's doing, good luck to him.

Next morning I'm getting ready to go to breakfast, and who walks into the mess in his uniform, that last night was in a bag behind a skip, but Spongey. "Sorry mate, I bottled it," he said, "but she's gonna come and see me in Bombay." How the hell had he gotten away with bringing a bin bag off the jetty back onto the ship is beyond me. Needless to say, I was not over the moon, given the risk I'd taken on his behalf, but in a funny way it was good to have him back on board.

Before we'd arrive in a new port, the Captain would come on the ship's tannoy and tell us bits and pieces about our new port of call. Arriving in Bombay, the most important thing he said was that Bombay would be unlike anywhere else we had visited on the trip and we should prepare ourselves for the level of poverty that we might be exposed to when we go ashore. He also advised not to venture anywhere near an area called the Cages.

We were all lined up in our white tropical uniform on the flight deck as we entered Bombay. The smell and the sound were unlike anything I'd ever experienced in my life. Also, in the dockyard, listing to one side and looking a shell of its former majestic self was HMS Hermes which the UK had sold to India. The last time I had seen her, she was tied up in Plymouth on the night I crossed the Tamar to join HMS Raleigh.

As soon as we were able, we left the ship and jumped into rickshaws. "Where to, boss?" the driver asked.

"The Cages," we all replied. Really not sure why the skipper made announcements about where not to go. We'd never heard of the Cages before he mentioned it as somewhere to avoid.

Having said that, I wished we'd listened to him. The place was hell on earth, a cesspit of human existence. We'd come from having spent a month in Australia, a vibrant, modern, beautiful country, to this. I'd never seen poverty and depravity like it. Children being offered to us for sex, people with some really grotesque skin diseases and disabilities just living on the street. It was just awful. We got out as quickly as our driver could peddle, avoiding the beggars and the cattle that roamed the streets.

Compare that to the splendour of the Taj Hotel near the Gateway to India. We spent many a night in there. One night a group of us were asked to leave because we got up and serenaded a female singer. We were all in our uniforms and we re-enacted the scene from Top Gun where they sing "You've Lost that

Loving Feeling." We thought we were hilarious, but it didn't go down all that well with hotel security.

Walking back to the dockyard from the Taj was always an interesting journey at night. You were constantly stepping over bodies just lying in the street or walking past someone taking a shit on the pavement. Wearing a white tropical uniform was never a great plan in Bombay. You could not help but want to give money to the young kids who were begging on the street. But these kids had it all worked out. They'd send the youngest and cutest kid to approach you first. But as soon as you gave him or her money, the rest of them appeared from nowhere, hundreds of them, and you'd be surrounded by all these kids who needed money. You only made that mistake once.

It was my first visit to India, and if I'm honest, I was glad to leave. Mainly because it meant we were on our way home, but also because I found it quite overwhelming. When I returned years later, I fell in love with the place, it's amazing. The people are so welcoming and will do anything for you.

We sailed back to the UK via Suez, stopping off at Gibraltar. My brother Paul flew out to Gibraltar and was able to sail back with us. I met him at the airport and brought him back to the ship. He was going to sleep in the bunk vacated by one of the lads who had flown home already as part of an advanced leave party. As Paul was sorting out his sleeping bag in the bunk space he found a discarded crusty sock down the side of the mattress. "Who's is this?" he asked.

"You don't wanna know, just put it in the bin." Poor lad.

We got back to the UK just before Christmas, 1988. It had been the most amazing six months of my life. So many amazing experiences, too many to recall here. I'd seen things I could only have dreamed about. The highlight was Sydney but when would I ever be in the Philippines or Singapore again in my life. I was 18 and had been halfway around the world. I think my decision not to stay on at Airbus was justified.

My time working in the ship's office because of the injury to my elbow also proved useful. I became aware of a different trade in the Navy and one to which I was better suited. Working as a Radar Operator was OK, but it wasn't stretching me at all. I'd developed a passion for learning that I never had at school. I had learnt that if you worked hard in the Navy, you could get promoted and earn more. Thankfully, the Navy recognised that I had some potential and agreed that I could retrain as a Ship's Writer. This would mean that I would be dealing with pay, foreign currency, correspondence and record keeping – essentially an Admin role but there were also some diverse opportunities within the field.

I left Ark Royal and returned to HMS Raleigh to undertake my writers' training. This was a 12-week course which I really enjoyed, and upon completion, I was sent to HMS Neptune in Faslane, Scotland. Neptune was the home of the UK's Nuclear deterrent and there was the permanent presence of a peace camp outside the gates. My lasting memory of Faslane is that it is always wet. I had never known a place like it for rain; it was permanently miserable. But like a lot of places, it was the people that made it, and I had some great times up there.

Being in Scotland gave me the opportunity to visit my Mum's brother Brian, whom l was close to. Uncle Brian lives in Langwathby just outside Penrith, so it was just over an hour from Glasgow Central. Brian is Mum's youngest brother and we both idolised H. He has been a huge support to me over the course of my life, and it is always great to spend time with him talking about my Grandad and the tales he used to tell of his experiences during the war. Being asked to be Godfather to Brian's first son, Simon, is one of the biggest honours of my life. Simon, of course, has followed the family tradition and joined the Navy. H would be so proud of us both and one of my other cousins, Jill, who also served.

Whilst at Faslane, I had my first experience of Scottish football and particularly the Old Firm. Like many English people, I suppose I had a view that outside of Celtic and Rangers, Scottish Football was pretty poor. If I had any allegiance, it was probably towards Celtic because there was a loose affinity between Everton and Celtic as being clubs historically associated with the Catholic Church. I wasn't a Catholic so that side of things wasn't important to me, but I used to wear a hat that was half Celtic and half Everton when they were popular at Goodison a few years earlier. I also owned a Celtic shirt, mainly because I liked the green-and-white style, and it was different. I remember Dad saying to me before I left for Scotland not to take the Celtic shirt with me because I would instantly alienate half of the population. How prophetic those words were!

Even in the office at Faslane, there was an animosity between Celtic and Rangers fans; it was really strange. Everton and Liverpool fans had their rivalry but would get together for a beer after a game; but with these guys it was proper hatred. I was given the opportunity to attend a Celtic game at Parkhead, my ticket was in a part of the ground called the Jungle. I went along and was excited to experience the atmosphere and to watch the game. Unfortunately, it was not a great experience. The atmosphere was horrible. The crowd were singing anti-British songs and revelling in pro-IRA chants and songs about hating the Queen. I felt distinctly uneasy all the way through. This wasn't a group of people that I felt any affinity to at all. They opposed everything that I realised I stood for. I couldn't wait to get out. I'd had my eyes opened to a side of football that I really didn't like.

A couple of weeks later, I was invited to Ibrox to watch a Rangers game. In the interest of balance, I was keen to go along and sample the other side of the rivalry. This, of course, was a very similar tribalistic experience except the views being expressed sat a lot more comfortably with who I was. This was all about the Union and the Queen, and very much anti-IRA. My job as a serviceman was not a problem here, nor my loyalty to the Queen, and it was a much more comfortable and enjoyable experience. Rangers were the top team in Scotland at the time and had recruited a couple of Everton players, after Everton had been barred from European competition thanks to the ban imposed after Heysel. I enjoyed watching Gary Stevens and Trevor Steven playing together again along with Iain Durrant, Mark Hateley and Derek Ferguson amongst others. Ibrox was also the best football stadium I had ever been in at that time. It never had the spiritual hold that Goodison had; at the end of the day, Rangers weren't my team, but it was a very impressive stadium at that time.

Glasgow is the only city I have been to (having never been to Belfast) where anyone who is interested would ascertain your religion within five minutes of meeting you, and potentially make a judgement or form an opinion of you. Your name, the school you went to, your address, your football allegiance; all paint a picture of who you are and what you're about. One Sunday afternoon, I was drinking in a bar in Helensburgh with a couple of friends from the base. We got talking football to some locals at the bar who were all Celtic supporters. It was a really good couple of hours sharing stories about our experience following our teams over the years. They talked about their dislike for Rangers and I was only too happy to talk about my dislike for Liverpool. I guess their allegiance to Celtic should have raised an alarm, but we were getting along so well, we didn't think it would matter that when asked what we were doing in Helensburgh, we informed them that we were in the Navy and worked at the base. The mood deteriorated immediately.

"See, yous… yous should be put on a raft and bombed by the fucking Provo's."

It wasn't just the guys that we were with that had turned hostile, the whole pub was now looking at us as if we were an enemy within. Two minutes earlier, we'd been talking about football but I was now very much fearing for my health.

"Get t'fuck oot of our town and d'nae come back you Brit bastards."

We didn't need to discuss their suggestion and left forthwith. A very surreal afternoon.

The Gulf War

I was not sorry to leave Faslane when the opportunity to work at Fleet Headquarters in Northwood came up. Northwood is located between Watford and London, and it presented a whole different lifestyle to what I'd experienced in the Navy before. I worked in the office of the Commander-in-Chief of the Fleet. I met people who hadn't been to sea for years, they'd gone from shore job to shore job, quite often not leaving Northwood. This wasn't quite the life I wanted at the age of 20, I'd done two years at sea on Ark Royal, retrained and wanted to get back to sea and I'd informed Naval Drafting that I would be a willing volunteer for a short-notice return to sea, if a ship became available.

Being at Northwood, however, gave me direct access to London and the opportunity to spend time in the Capital and all it had to offer. Wembley was a couple of stops away on the tube, and I was able to meet lads from home who had come down to watch Tranmere Rovers in the 1990 play-off Final. It was a very different world from what I'd experienced in Scotland, and I was working with a very different side of the Navy. That summer was amazing. The World Cup was in Italy and England made it to the semi-finals. It was Gazza's tournament and the atmosphere across the country was awesome. At Northwood, we would all congregate in the bar, watch the games and then the party would start. I would wake up in the WRNS quarters more often than I should have, and would then have to sneak out in the morning to go and get showered and changed into uniform to go to work, often having had very little sleep. Such was the life of a young sailor who was grabbing every opportunity to live life.

On Friday, 31st August 1990, I was sitting at my desk, working away, when our office manager, a Warrant Officer, shouted over, "Martin, you still looking to get back to sea?"

"Yes, sir," I replied.

"Very good; you'll be joining HMS London on Sunday evening and sailing to the Gulf on Monday." How quickly life can change. The rest of that day was a bit of a whirlwind.

Saddam Hussein had recently invaded Kuwait and the US, UK and some of the Gulf states were forming a coalition in order to remove his forces, by force if necessary. London was due to sail to the Gulf anyway as part of the Royal Navy's Armilla patrol which saw a British warship patrolling the Gulf waters to protect British shipping in the area. However, the way things were escalating, it was clear that this was going to be no ordinary Gulf deployment.

That afternoon I was issued a new respirator (gas mask) that I needed to test and make sure that the face seal was correct. Then it was down to the medical centre for a couple of top-up vaccinations. I then went back to my room, packed everything into my kitbag and made my way to Watford station to catch a train home to see Mum and Dad and Paul for a day, before heading down to Plymouth to join the ship.

On the morning of 3rd September, we spent a few hours loading last-minute provisions required for our deployment. Seeing body bags being received on board certainly provided a focus on what might lay ahead. That was a very strange experience. I remember wondering whether one of them would be mine, and how many body bags would actually be needed. Very sobering thoughts. We set sail from Plymouth, not knowing what the next six months would have in store for us.

I can't say that I'd given much thought to the UK being involved in conflict up until this point. Of course, when you join the military, there is always the possibility that you will be called upon, should such a situation arise. This was our time and I, for one, was really looking forward to it.

When we left Plymouth, there was nothing certain about whether we would enter hostilities, as political and diplomatic resolutions were being sought. We used the passage from Plymouth to the Gulf to prepare ourselves for whatever the next six months would bring.

The UN had already imposed sanctions on Iraq, and part of our role, when we arrived on station, would be to enforce those sanctions. The role of the Navy would be to stop Iraqi merchant shipping entering the Gulf, carrying supplies to help Saddam's war machine. This task had already commenced, and it would be our role to replace the British Navy ships who were coming to the end of their deployment in the Gulf. In addition to that, HMS London would be the Flag Ship for the Royal Navy's ever-growing group of ships and minesweepers heading east. Our group of ships was known as group X-Ray and comprised of the Type

22 Frigate *Brazen,* The Type 42 Destroyers *Cardiff* and *Gloucester* and ourselves, another Type 22 Frigate.

It's hard to imagine now, given everything that has happened in Iraq and the Middle East as a whole since the early '90s, but at the time that Saddam Hussain invaded Kuwait, he commanded the 4th biggest Army in the world and the 5th largest air force. The Iraqi Army had been involved in a 10-year battle against their neighbours Iran, so there was no doubt that they would be ready for a fight. Iraq also had an array of anti-ship weapons including 50 Mirage Fighter – Bombers, 400 air-launched Exocet missiles along with 7 shore launchers with 50 Silkworm anti-ship missiles. In addition to that, and as we were soon to find out, they owned a whole load of sea mines.

Their war with Iran had shown that they were not afraid to start throwing chemical weapons around. Many of Iraq's weapons were capable of delivering chemical substances such as mustard gas. Mustard gas was used in the 1st World War and causes blistering of the skin and lungs, allowing nerve agents an easier passage into the body and the central nervous system. If he was prepared to use chemical weapons, then we had to assume that he would also be prepared to use biological weapons too. By polluting the water supply with Anthrax or Bubonic Plague, for example, he could infect thousands of people. The thought of being involved in a chemical or biological war was sobering, to say the least.

We practised and drilled every scenario imaginable. Air attacks, missile hits, gas attacks, mine strikes – you name it, we practised it. The more we practiced the better we got with our reactions. Our practices increased in intensity in the period before Christmas. Having to deal with the aftermath of a chemical attack and multiple casualties was a sobering thought but a scenario that we needed to be prepared for. We'd done all this before of course during exercises or during training but there is nothing like a real threat to focus the mind. I can't speak for everyone on board, but my biggest worry was the threat of chemical weapons attack. Although to be fair, when you think about it, if I was going to die at sea, there's no preferred way to go, burning, drowning, blown to bits, it was never going to be pleasant.

Some of my new shipmates had served in the Falklands eight years earlier and did not share the enthusiasm of us younger sailors to get into the action. In fact, some suffered badly with PTSD when our drills and exercises were ramped up. If anything, this gave me a bit of a wake-up call about what we were potentially heading into. Most of those guys had wives and children back home, which was a consideration that I never had, and I just couldn't understand what they would have been feeling as we headed closer to the Gulf.

As we sailed around the Gulf of Oman, we moved into what was called Defence Watches. Usually, ships operated a 7-watch system over a 24-hour period.

Forenoon – 8 am–12 pm
Afternoon – 12 pm–4 pm
1st Dog – 4 pm–6 pm
2nd Dog – 6 pm–8 pm
First – 8 pm –12 pm
Middle – 12 am–4 am
Morning – 4 am–8 am

In Defence watches, everyone worked a straight 6 on/6 off. This would be our war footing should hostilities commence, and so there was no harm in getting into the routine now. Besides which, we were shortly to sail through the Straits of Hormuz, a strategically significant stretch of water between Iran and the UAE. The Strait is around 90nm long and at its narrowest point is 21nm wide. A third of the world's liquefied natural gas and almost 25% of total global oil consumption passed through the strait. As a result of its strategic importance, the area is often a location for tension between East and West. It had been targeted by Iraq in the Iran/Iraq war in the 1980s with the Iraqi's looking for Iran to close the strait, which would, in turn, have had an international impact and likely led to U.S. intervention.

It was well known that Iranian military installations at Bandar Abbas tracked all shipping heading into the Gulf including UK and U.S. warships.

Once on station in the Gulf, we soon slipped into routine. Eight days out at sea followed by 4 days alongside for maintenance etc. We visited many different ports in the Gulf in the period before Christmas, Jebel Ali, Port Rashid, Bahrain, Abu Dhabi and Sharjah to name a few. Being at sea in the Gulf was enjoyable. The sea was always pretty calm and the sun beat down day after day. Dolphins would often accompany the ship, criss-crossing across the bow as we made our passage. Yellow sea-snakes were always visible on the surface of the water and flying fish provided a spectacular show whenever they appeared. I always found the tranquillity of being on the upper deck, looking out to sea, very relaxing but there was always something to remind me that trouble was brewing; be it the sight of another warship or a formation of fighter aircraft passing by overhead.

Weeks and months passed by without a diplomatic resolution, and the likelihood of military action grew ever more real. On 29th November 1990, the UN Security Council gave Saddam until 16th January 1991 to withdraw his forces from Kuwait. A date had been set and this focussed the mind somewhat. We now had a timescale and the countdown to action began.

We had been ordered to sleep above the waterline on the ship because of the threat of mines. Saddam had released mines into the Gulf that would move southwards using the current. Some were the familiar sea mines that were round and had spikes coming out of them that bobbed along on the seas surface. More of a threat though, were the magnetic mines that floated underneath the surface, waiting for a ship to sail over them before rising and exploding on contact. Clearly, these were a bit of a hindrance as they could not be seen. The presence of these hidden killers meant that we were never able to truly relax at sea. They were a real threat every minute of every day for the period of time that we were at sea.

Our messdecks were all low down in the ship and therefore below the waterline, and whilst moving to another location to sleep was obviously the right thing to do, spending months sleeping on a desk in the ship's office was not fun. The precaution was proved right though on February 19th, 1991, when two American ships that we were operating with, USS Tripoli and USS Princeton, were both hit by mines. The power of the explosions were felt onboard our ship as the blast waves dispersed.

Being on station in the Gulf in the run up to conflict also brought about different daily routines. We were told to organise what was known as a battle bag which we would have to carry around with us everywhere we went. The battle bag included more protective clothing, anti-flash hood and gloves, chemical defence kit and epi-pen and our respirators (gas masks). The other essential items to be carried at all times were your mug and some eating irons. If we were to get called to action stations for a period of time, the mug was essential to ensure that when the cooks came round with a brew or some soup, you were able to take advantage.

Of course, with the temperatures being as they are out in that part of the world, it was not always a pleasurable experience wearing all this gear and lugging it round everywhere you went. The thought of needing to fight in it all was not appealing. There was already an aroma about the ship and cleanliness and personal hygiene were essential. Wearing our gas masks for any length of time was uncomfortable. Not because of how they fitted but because of the heat and sweat that built up inside them, taking them off introduced you to a smell of slimy, wet rubber. It was pretty disgusting as I remember.

Christmas 1990 was spent alongside in Jebel Ali, a huge port complex outside Dubai. Jebel Ali was, at the time, the world's biggest man-made harbour; it was huge and made the Naval Dockyards in Portsmouth and Devonport look tiny.

One of the biggest concerns we had around this time was whether or not Saddam would make a preemptive strike against the coalition. He knew the date of the UN ultimatum and he also knew that any strike against the coalition around Christmas would be a huge propaganda coup for him, and could easily weaken the resolve of the public in the U.S, UK and France to support action. Another fear that our politicians and Commanders had was that Saddam could launch a missile strike on Israel in an attempt to goad them into a retaliatory strike that would thereby pit the Jews against the Arabs. The U.S. and the UK did not want this situation to arise because it had the potential to split the coalition with Arab states not wanting to side with the Jewish state. It was a political hot potato to say the least.

It was in this atmosphere of anxiety and the unknown that we entered Christmas 1990. Those of you who know Dubai as it is now, will not recognise the Dubai that we frequented back in 1990. I was able to take a day's leave over Christmas and, with a couple of mates, checked into the Chicago Beach Hotel on Christmas Eve.

Chicago Beach was located off a dirt road that ran between old town Bur Dubai and Jebel Ali. It was a huge hotel and we found it occupied by stranded aircrew whose airlines had stopped flying in and out of the region as the build-up of troops continued. Chicago Beach is now called Jumeirah Beach and the hotel is now the Jumeirah Beach Hotel and looks very different. Having been back to Dubai many times since the end of the Gulf War, it is hard to recognise the place. In fact, the only area that I can remember is the creek and the Dhows that sail up and down and the Gold Souk.

The Gulf News newspaper ran regular features on the region's new visitors, and one day, several lads off the British ships were invited to go and meet Miss Russia and have a photoshoot. Quite what she was doing in Dubai was anybody's guess, but when asked to go along, I was only too pleased. If this is what Her Majesty's Navy required of me, then I was duty bound to oblige. Clearly, word had gotten around the fleet of my appearance in Aussie Vogue. Fair play, Miss Russia was stunning; very, very pretty. Didn't speak a word of the Queen's though and conversation was minimal. After a few months of celibacy, sitting next to such a beautiful girl did none of us any good whatsoever.

We used to go and drink in hotel bars; there were only a few of them that sold alcohol then. The Ramada used to be a favourite, and there was another hotel that housed Thatcher's Bar downstairs and another popular haunt was a place called Pancho Villas. These bars were always full of British and American sailors. We found the Americans much more gung-ho than we were. We were much more matter-of-fact and down to earth, and I got the sense that the Americans were just very different in their approach to things than us.

Christmas Eve and Christmas Day were spent on the Beach. I seem to remember drinking a lot of rum. It was the first Christmas that I'd ever spent away from home. I was on a deserted beach in the sun and it couldn't have felt less like Christmas. We left Dubai on Boxing Day morning and would not return until March.

Sometime around 8th January, we received a very special visitor to the ship. Prime Minister John Major had been in post a matter of days following the ousting of Margaret Thatcher.

Some of the ship's company were asked to congregate in the ship's dining room and the Prime Minister was introduced to us all. I'm not sure it was particularly memorable for either me or Mr Major. We shook hands but didn't chat. I met him again in 2018 at Lord's, he remembered visiting the ship, but it was clear that I had left very little impression on him.

Two weeks into the New Year, no diplomatic answer had been found. Saddam refused the requested, unconditional withdrawal of his troops from Kuwait. Military intervention from the coalition forces was now a question of when rather than if. All of us onboard HMS London and, no doubt, the other ships in the Gulf at the time were wearing white, anti-flash overalls instead of our normal No 8 working clothes. We carried our anti-gas respirators everywhere with us as well as anti-flash hoods and gloves. Our skipper was receiving information from the Government and was preparing us, as best as he could, for an imminent escalation in events.

We had been taking NAPs Tablets (Nerve Agent Prophylactic) every four hours to prepare our bodies in case we became exposed to chemical weapons. One day, we were told that we needed to have some more injections that would help protect us if we came under chemical attack. There wasn't a discussion about this, we were left in no doubt that we had to have these injections for our own good. I remember having a number of different injections on the same day and was advised that they were to strengthen or protect our nervous systems in the event of chemical attack. Two of them were for Anthrax and Plague. We didn't think anything of it. If that was what we needed to do to protect ourselves, then so be it. It wasn't until sometime after we returned home that we began to question the wisdom of having taken these drugs.

The UN resolution expired at midday Gulf time on 16th January. At 0300 on the morning of 17th January, the ship's alarm sounded and we were called to Action Stations. This is the condition where the ship is ready to fight. I remember jumping out of bed, well off my desk, never having moved so fast in all my life. The ship was alive with everybody rushing to their point of duty. I was laughing hysterically, a very bizarre reaction when heading into something so potentially dangerous. As I was climbing a ladder, I saw one of my mates whose eyes looked shot – I could see the tension and worry in his face. Why was I reacting differently to him? I didn't have time to dwell on it. Adrenaline is a funny thing; I'm guessing I was high on it. I've never experienced anything like that buzz before or since. I found it fascinating to see how adrenaline affected different people.

We all know that adrenaline is a hormone produced by our bodies as reaction to a stimulus such as a threat, stress or excitement. It enables the body to react rapidly in a fight-or-flight situation. It enables oxygen to get to our lungs and muscles quicker and allows our brains to think more quickly. It also increases our pain threshold. The release of adrenaline as a response to a threat is almost immediate, within seconds, hence the term Adrenaline rush.

The release of adrenaline was causing changes in my body that I had no understanding of how to control. I'd never had an experience like this before. I now recognise that what I was experiencing was a high caused by the release of the adrenaline in response to the situation that we were in.

The opening exchanges of battle and the uncertainty of the enemy's capability to respond whether with general firepower or chemical weapons is not a situation or an environment that many would choose to associate with, or be part of. Yet there I was, 20 years old, thinking I was indestructible and feeling as if I was loving every minute of it. It is amazing how our bodies adapt in order to protect us from ourselves sometimes. As I reflect on my experience now, I can understand that I was naïve; I was high on a hormone released to enable me to cope with a very unusual set of circumstances. It didn't make me better able to deal with the situation than anyone else. It enabled me to deal with it in my way. It was clearly the most stressful situation that I'd ever experienced in my young life up until that point, but the amazing human body adapted and made sure that I was ready for whatever was about to come our way.

Every person on a warship has a role to play when the ship is called into action. Some are first-aiders to deal with casualties, some were fire fighters, some manned the guns, others worked in the Operations Room. The Ops Room is where the ship fights from, it is where the Captain locates himself and is the focal point for all of the information coming into the ship from signals, intercepts, radar and sonar. My role was to record information coming back from firefighting parties at the forward end of the ship. They would provide feedback to me regarding which compartments had been damaged by fire, or were taking in water after a missile hit. They'd tell me how many casualties they'd found; my job was to prioritise which information was passed up the chain of command to ensure that the senior officers onboard were able to make the right decisions in order to save the ship and its crew. It was a great role. Thankfully, I only had to fulfil it during exercises, but that morning we were all ready to go and awaiting an update from the skipper.

He eventually announced that hostilities had commenced against Iraq. U.S. ships in the Gulf were launching Tomahawk missiles as he spoke and they were flying through the air above us. We had to remain on alert for any retaliatory strike from Iraq. I found it exhilarating.

After about six hours, we were stood down from action stations and we reverted back into defence watches.

On 23rd January, HMS London was positioned close to the Saudi shoreline. We were called to Action Stations as Radar had picked up three Scud missiles travelling towards us from deep in Iraq. Air Raid Warning Red is the state when an air attack is imminent. We knew these missiles were heading south but we were unsure of their intended target. A few moments later, the target was identified as Dharan airbase, a few miles from us on the Saudi coast. From my position inside the ship, I was unable to witness the firework display as two of the Scuds were taken out by the American Patriot missile system. The third missile apparently overshot its target an exploded harmlessly in the sea not far from us.

At 0925 the next morning, the alarm went again. "Air Raid Warning Red, Action Stations Action Stations." Fast moving contacts to the north west had been identified as Iraqi Mirage jets and they were heading towards us. Unless you are working in the Ops Room on the ship, you're pretty much oblivious to what's going on, except for when someone makes an announcement. So, you man your action station and nervously wait for an update. On this occasion, proceedings ended quite quickly as the two jets picked up on radar were met by coalition fighters and swiftly did a U-turn. However, they were high-level decoys for two other fighters, flying at a much lower level, carrying Exocet missiles and seeking to attack allied warships. These were picked up and shot down by coalition fighters before they could release their missiles. It's fair to say that things were lively, and of course there was the constant threat from mines.

Over the next few weeks, we were in and out of Action Stations on numerous occasions. Mainly this was when the Iraqis fired either Scud or Silkworm missiles from their positions on land. The Iraqis were trying to hit the large U.S. battleships, Wisconsin and Missouri, who were using their large guns to shell Iraqi positions on land. HMS London and HMS Gloucester were positioned between the shore and the U.S. battleships so that our antiair missile systems could take out any Iraqi missiles heading towards the U.S. ships. It was a precarious position, we had U.S. shells going overhead in one direction and Iraqi missiles coming towards us in the other direction. For the most part, we were untroubled by the Iraqis, but on one occasion, HMS Gloucester used her missiles to take out an Iraqi missile that was heading for us. We were called to Action Stations once our radar had picked up the launch of the missile and the ships tannoy system gave us a countdown of the trajectory and distance away from us. Fair to say, for a minute or two, it was squeaky bum time as the missile closed on our position. Gloucester's missile system had a longer range than ours, so it was always going to be them that took the first attempt to take it out. There was a palpable sense of relief when the news came over the tannoy that the inbound missile had been "splashed".

Despite the odd missile attack, by far the biggest threat to us were the mines. The Gulf was full of them and before we could make any progress north towards Kuwait and Iraq, we had to wait for mine sweepers to clear a channel so that we could follow them north. It was slow work and they could not afford to get it wrong. Whilst it wasn't surprising that the two American ships were hit by mines, after all there were so many of them, we couldn't work out how it had happened because we were all in a convoy behind the mine sweepers. The only conclusion that we could come to was that the Americans had tried to cut a corner and paid the price. Those two ships were immediately ahead of us in the convoy and its certainly focussed the mind when the first one got hit, closely followed by the second. We heard and felt the explosions below decks and for a while, we were waiting for one of those magnetic mines to strike us. Thankfully, it never happened.

The threat of being struck by a mine was constant for the duration of our patrol in the Gulf. Our helicopter scanned the area around us, daily plotting the position of surface mines. They could be avoided but the biggest danger were the magnetic ones. The minesweepers did an amazing job clearing safe channels through which we could pass, but with the constant threat of mines, attacks from shore-based missiles and sleeping on or under a desk for weeks on end, it was clear that this was not an ordinary tour of duty.

The Iraqis surrendered on 28th February, a little over a month since the start of the coalition hostilities. They had been completely annihilated on land and their air force became non-existent within the first week, giving the coalition free reign in the skies. When I eventually managed to get outside on the upper deck, there was no sun. The sky was grey and thick with acrid smoke from where Saddam's forces had set the oil fields of Kuwait on fire. Visibility wasn't great but you could clearly see the fires and the plumes of black smoke rising from the oil fields. Some days the smoke was so bad that you couldn't even make out whether it was daytime or night time. The smoke filled the air. It was environmental sabotage on an enormous scale.

HMS Beaver, a Type 22 frigate, came out to the Gulf to take over from us. Someone at the Admiralty had a sense of humour because HMS Beaver was the first warship sent out to the region to have females on board as members of the ship's company. The irony of the name and its crew was not lost on anybody, and on the day we did our handover and sailed close to Beaver in the Gulf, one of our crew unfurled a bed sheet with, "Welcome to the Gulf to the Beaver on the Beaver," written on it. Our ship's company were in stitches but I'm not so sure our skipper or theirs were over the moon about it.

There is lots written about the impact of war and conflict. I have to be honest and say that my experience was nowhere near as extreme as, say the soldiers on land, or the RAF fighter pilots who were shot down and held captive. We had our moments at sea, as I mentioned earlier, and living for months with the constant threat of hitting a mine was not great.

Worrying about the threat of chemical attack is far better than experiencing it. I was 20 years old, I had no responsibilities, and I was ridiculously naïve. I found the experience exciting and I loved the adrenalin buzz when we got called to Action Stations. I don't recall being scared or frightened by what we were experiencing; like I said I was naïve.

The thought of getting home was all-consuming. I was looking forward to getting home and down to the Mercia for a pint with Dad. I'd missed a decent pint of Guinness, all we had access to in the Gulf was overpriced Heineken or whatever we were given on board.

It is only now that I have children of my own that I can begin to imagine what my mum and dad were going through whilst I was out there. I also had the opportunity to say no and not join HMS London when I was asked. Sometimes you just have to take the opportunities that life throws at you. I was, and to a degree still am, very single-minded. If I want to do something, then you're welcome to come along but if not, I'll see you later. At the time that I said I'd join London, I didn't know that she was sailing to the Gulf, and there was no guarantee that there would be conflict anyway because the hope in September 1990 was that the conflict would be resolved diplomatically. But I said yes to the opportunity given to me, and I experienced an event that gave me a very different perspective on life as I grew older. Military service is brilliant at taking you out of your comfort zone, it makes you rise to challenges that you might ordinarily pass by. It developed me because being out of your comfort zone and experiencing new things is fertile land and you can't help but grow as a person when exposed to such challenges.

I got home in the middle of March. Mum told me that she knew I was coming home because a lady had stopped her in the street in Chester and told her not to worry and that I would be safe and home very soon. It was not for the first time Mum had one of these experiences. I'm not sure how much I believed in such things, but Mum certainly did.

The first few nights at home were a bit strange. I was waking up at ridiculous hours of the morning, looking for my NAPS tablets to take. Then Mum and Dad had this alarm clock that sounded very similar to the ship's general alarm to call us to Action Stations. It went off at 6:30 in the morning for Dad to get up for work. As he was stumbling out of bed, I had shot up and was looking for my respirator, ready to go to Action Stations. Being home took a lot of getting used to.

Looking back, my experience in the Gulf gave me perspective. I don't worry about too much and I definitely operate better when under pressure. But how do you learn such things about yourself until you have been under pressure? I didn't realise it at the time but those six months out in the Gulf taught me so much and shaped my character.

I didn't feel as if I had anything in common with anybody anymore other than my mates in the Navy. They were my family now. I'd become institutionalised in a major way and I was more than happy with my life as it was pretty much mapped out until I reached the age of 40. Looking back now, I think I let myself down on more than one occasion. I'd become quite selfish and pretty much did whatever I wanted and didn't worry too much about consequences. There is a part of a sailor's life that can descend into, what I would describe as, being feral. I inhabited that space for a while after returning home from the Gulf. The problem was, it became the norm because when I was in Plymouth or later on up in Scotland again, I was with a group of mates that worked hard and played harder. We would drink far too much but we were loving life. We were more roguish than troublemakers. I can't ever remember being in trouble with either the civilian police or the Navy police, although I did end up in the back of a police car one night.

In Helensburgh, near Faslane, there was a great Chinese restaurant that we all used to head to after drinking in the local bars. The restaurant was up a steep flight of stairs from the street. One night, we'd finished our food and it was gone 1 in the morning, and we needed to head back to the base. As I got to the top of the stairs to go down on to the street to call a taxi, I looked down; and as luck would have it, a taxi was right outside. "Lads, Strathclyde Taxis outside," I yelled as I made my way down the stairs and jumped into the back of the car. "Two minutes mate, a couple more coming and then back to the base please." It was at this point that the driver turned around and suggested in a quite a gruff but forceful tone that I might like to "get the f**k out of the car or else I'd end up in a cell". I left the vehicle in haste to realise that the sign on the side of the car read Strathclyde Police and not Strathclyde Taxis. Didn't live that one down for a while.

Playing for Time

The start of my eventual discharge from the Navy began in the summer of 1991. I was playing football with lads off the ship at the shore base HMS Drake in Plymouth. The ankle that I damaged in basic training 4 years earlier was still giving me gyp from time to time, but nothing I couldn't put up with. Clearly, there was a weakness there and as I put my right foot down to cross the ball with my left, the ankle rolled again. I was in absolute agony.

I was on crutches for a while and therefore unable to serve at sea. I was removed from HMS London and sent on sick leave prior to joining HMS Neptune again up at Faslane in Scotland. Whilst I was away in the Gulf, the Navy had begun making enquiries as to my suitability to hold, what they called, Enhanced Positive Vetting – essentially this was to make sure that I was not a security risk and that I could be drafted to work in highly classified environments and handle state secrets. With this process completed, I was informed that I would spend the next three years at a base called RAF Edzell near Brechin in Scotland, starting in January 1992.

For this post, I was required to drive, and the Navy arranged driving lessons for me. So, in New Year 1992, I went to Portsmouth to begin my Navy Driving Course. I started on a Monday and had my first test on the Friday. I failed because the instructor reckoned that I cut someone up on a roundabout. I resat the test the following Monday and passed. So, with all of one week's driving experience, I went home, bought a car and drove five hours up the motorway to Edzell.

It was whilst I was up in Scotland that I received an appointment to attend the Royal Navy's hospital at Haslar in Gosport, Hampshire. They had decided that my ankle was indeed in need of repair. So, in the summer of 1992, I packed a bag and reported to RNH Haslar for an operation to repair my very strained ankle ligaments. The procedure was called an "Evans" procedure which involved drilling a hole in the ankle bone and passing the ligament through the hole and tying it to the muscles underneath. I was operated on by Mr Farquharson-Roberts, known by everybody as MFR. He was one of the Queen's surgeons. I had every confidence that this was going to sort my problems out once and for all. MFR explained that my lateral ankle ligament was essentially a waste of time. It had been stretched so far by repeated twisting/turning that it would not repair itself and return to its usual length, hence the need to tighten it up through surgery.

The operation went well, and MFR was happy. I was discharged within the week and sent back up to Scotland for six weeks in plaster and to begin my rehab. I was under the care of the Chief Medic at 40 Commando Royal Marines, based in Arbroath, about 20 miles from Edzell. He was a lovely bloke and he lined me up with the physios at Stracathro Hospital, which was literally a five-minute drive from Edzell. As soon as the plaster came off, I was straight into physio.

It was then that things started to unravel for me. The physio was not happy with the progress that I was making in terms of regaining muscle strength. She could see that I was putting the work in but she said that the muscle strength was not returning in the way that she would've expected to see. She referred me to a Neurological Consultant at Ninewells Hospital in Dundee.

It was now early 1993 and whilst awaiting my consultant's appointment, life carried on as normal. I really enjoyed life at Edzell. I was living off base, sharing a cottage with a mate and we just had a riot. As soon as we clocked off on a Friday, the party began. We'd head straight into Brechin, have an Indian for dinner and then head to the local pubs. The most popular being a place called Amigo's which was on the corner of the high street. We loved it there, we were on first-name terms with the bar staff and we were well looked after. There was never any hassle, we lost hours, if not days and weekends, in that place.

I say there was never any hassle. Edzell was a U.S. Navy base, there were 3000 U.S. Navy and Marines stationed there alongside 40 of us British. The bar was like something you'd expect in any American town, serving Bud, Coors and many different types of Bourbon. Like any reasonable sized American community, there were many with Irish heritage. This was the early 1990s, the Good Friday agreement was still some years away and the IRA were active both in Northern Ireland and on the mainland. So you can imagine the reaction of us Brits one St Patricks night when one of the U.S. sailors started walking around the bar with a bag, asking for donations to "the cause". "What cause is that then?" we asked.

"Ah just for my brothers and sisters in the struggle in Ireland," came the reply. Talk about lighting the blue touch paper. He was left with a very clear understanding of what the struggle meant for British servicemen. The ignorance was unbelievable.

My appointment with the consultant came around and I found myself lying on a hospital bed with a Dr attaching electric wires to my leg. One, a transmitter at the top of the nerve near my knee, the other, a receiver, at the bottom of the nerve near my ankle. This, as I would later become very familiar with, was a nerve conduction study. I had no idea what they were testing for. All I knew was that the physio wasn't happy with my muscle strength following my operation. I learnt that they were measuring the speed that an electric pulse travels via my nerve between the point of transmission and the point of reception. The results tell them how well my nerves are transmitting signals from the brain. It really isn't a very nice thing to undertake. They measured conductivity with different strengths of pulse. Fair play, it hurt.

After the tests had finished, the consultant came over and told me what they'd found, namely a delay in the transmission of the pulse. Therefore, the muscles only receive a weakened signal and believe that they aren't being stimulated so they waste – if you don't use them, you lose them. "Tell me," he said, "do any of your family have trouble walking?" I told him about my dad. "There you are, you've got Charcot Marie Tooth syndrome."

I'd never heard of this condition, but he went on to tell me that it is hereditary and can pass from generation to generation, and that it will gradually get worse as I get older. It's a condition that affects the nerves and their ability to transmit signals to the muscles. I was lying on the bed in utter disbelief of what I was hearing. I was listening to this guy that I'd never even met an hour ago, telling me that I had a condition that I'd never heard of, and that it had been given to me by my dad. What's more is that it is going to get worse as I get older. A realisation hit me there and then, that my job would be at risk when the Navy would find out. I had so many questions: *Why me? Why now?* And also, given that I didn't have these problems 12 months ago, what impact had the drugs that I was given in the Gulf, had on my nervous system. He couldn't answer that because he wasn't a military surgeon, but there was something about this whole thing that I didn't like and I couldn't get my head around. I'd never felt so alone as I did in that hospital on that day. My world had collapsed. Things were never going to be the same after this diagnosis. I also now had information about the condition that my dad didn't have. I had the diagnosis that he'd been searching for.

It was explained to me that the condition can present itself in different ways in different people, even within the same family. All the times that I'd had people taking the piss out of my skinny legs or my funny run or my slapping feet – did I have this condition all along?

He explained that, potentially, I could have been a carrier of the gene and that something may have happened to trigger the onset in me. He felt it unlikely that I'd have been fit enough at 16 to have joined the Navy had it been presenting at that stage. Which raised the question for me of the impact of the drugs we were given in the Gulf.

Many servicemen who had returned from the Gulf were reporting health defects, both in themselves and in children that had been born since their return, and I was now being told that I had a condition that impacts on my nervous system, having been given drugs that affected my nerves. It was far too coincidental in my view. I have to accept the fact that I may have been carrying the gene anyway, but for me to have deteriorated as much as I had, and so quickly, made me wonder what impact the drugs given in the Gulf had had.

A train of events was now set in place which would see me leave the Navy a year later. Firstly, a report of my diagnosis was sent to the Chief Doc at 40 Commando Royal Marines. I explained to him my concerns about the drugs given to me in the Gulf, and he requested my medical records. It turned out that they had been lost or destroyed – there was nothing for him to look at and no record of the injections that I was given.

My fitness to serve was now in doubt and that was reflected on my records. I had been medically downgraded which in turn would impact on how the Navy could use me. I had volunteered to serve in Northern Ireland as my next posting, again making use of the vetting process that I had been through. Slowly but surely, different doors were being closed on me. It just seemed absolutely bonkers that the Navy had invested so much in me in terms of training and the vetting process, and I, in turn, had gained quick promotion and had passed exams to be promoted again; yet all the discussion was about fitness to serve at sea when I would not have been due at sea for at least another eight years. They didn't need to lecture me about being able to go to sea at a moment's notice – I fulfilled that part of the deal in September 1990 when I joined HMS London at a moment's notice. There seemed to be a lack of logic and common sense and I felt like a victim of it. That said, this was still a Navy that was kicking out homosexuals, so those with medical conditions didn't stand much of a chance.

By early 1994, we had built up a case for my retention within the Service that we felt was strong. I certainly couldn't have asked for more support from Graham Churton, my boss at Edzell. I knew that my career within the Navy was going to look different from what I had hoped, but I thought that an exemplary Service record and glowing references and recommendations from my boss might hold some sway. So, when I went down to Haslar to stand in front of the Medical Board of Survey, I was confident that common sense may prevail.

Three weeks later, my world fell apart. I left the Navy very bitter and very angry at the way that I'd been treated. I'd given everything to my Navy career. They had diagnosed a disability, given me no support following that diagnosis, and subsequently made me feel useless to them. Everything that I had achieved and the service that I had provided, counted for absolutely nothing. They released me back into a world where I was a nobody. I'd lost my confidence and my identity. Yesterday, I was Ian Martin, Royal Navy; today I was Ian Martin, no job and absolutely no idea which way to turn. It was the single worst experience of my life and it didn't end on the day I left.

At the start of your Service career, the Armed Forces spend the first six weeks institutionalising you into life in the military. They invest time and energy into ensuring that you fit the bill and that they are happy to let you into their world. You aren't allowed to go home during this period of time and any individuality that you display when you arrive is moulded into what is acceptable within your new world.

When you leave, there is no such preparation to readjust you to civvy street. I found it a very rude awakening. Talk about being a fish out of water – I was a whale out of the ocean and floundering on the beach. My life felt really empty. The security blanket of the Navy had gone. I was barely more than a child when I joined up at 16. The Navy replaced my parents, they gave me structure to my life and added a bit of discipline. They fed me and made sure I always had a bed to return to, even if some nights I never quite made it for one reason or another. They paid me reasonably well and provided a surrogate family of likeminded people with whom I identified and felt comfortable with. They say that the friends you make in the forces are friends for life. I'm not sure I agree with that. Because of the transient nature of life in the Navy, you move on every couple of years. I made a shitload of acquaintances, but very few friends. That said, for the period of time you are with people, you are like a band of brothers. You'll do anything for your mates. I missed that. The Navy gave me an identity that I never had as a young adolescent growing up in a small village in North Wales. I developed a sense of my place in the world and also how big the world was, both physically and metaphorically. I learned lessons that school can't teach you. GCSE Welsh wouldn't have saved me from the little Phillipino chap and his machete chasing me through Olongapo City. Algebra wouldn't have helped me had we been hit by a missile or a mine in the Gulf. That said, I'm not sure that passing the Naval swimming test at the umpteenth time of asking actually helped me either, because the first sink-or-swim situation that I found myself in was when I became a civvy – and I was struggling to stay afloat.

Returning to civvy street felt as strange as my first few weeks at HMS Raleigh. The difference being that I wasn't with 25 other blokes going through the same thing. I was very much on my own, I couldn't find anyone who could relate to my situation. I'd lost my sense of purpose; I was angry and struggling.

The Middle Order

I moved back home to North Wales, arguably the worst decision of my life. It seems obvious to me now but at the time I didn't understand what was going on. The Navy had been a surrogate family to me from the age of 16. It provided structure, routine, discipline and security during the most impressionable years of my life. It had shaped who I was, it rewarded me for hard work by way of promotion and it gave me values and behaviours that I still live by today. I can see all this now but, in the Spring of 1994, aged 24, I had no idea who I was anymore.

I needed time to figure out what had happened and to choose what direction I needed to go in. In some ways I was in a good position, I'd had the best part of nine years military experience, I was disciplined and could be relied upon – all the things that you might expect from an ex-serviceman. I had the opportunity to start again, my Navy experience was in the bank and in a way, the world was my oyster. I wanted to take time to decide what path to travel next as I'd only have this one opportunity to start again, rushing into something now would potentially cause problems down the line.

I was trying to think rationally and make sensible choices. I didn't realise it at the time but inside I was crying. To be fair to Mum and Dad, they took me back in and ensured I had a roof over my head, but we had very different thoughts on what I should do next. Dad would come home from work with the local paper, having circled jobs that he thought that I should apply for. I would look at them and feel dismayed that he thought I was only good enough for labouring or production line jobs. Not that there is anything wrong with those jobs, but I thought I'd made it clear when I joined the Navy that those roles weren't for me, just not what I wanted to do. The very thought of me taking a bit of time to figure out my next move was lost on him. In his mind, I had become a slacker and a layabout, and he wasn't shy about letting me know.

It is clear to me now that I came back home because home would be the place where I would feel the most secure given what had happened. Subconsciously, my mind had steered me that way because one of our most basic needs as humans is to feel secure. What I hadn't bargained on was the lack of empathy and understanding that I encountered from those closest to me.

I think this is where the pain of the Navy's handling of my situation continued. I thought that by coming back home, I'd get the support and love that I badly needed at the lowest point of my life. It didn't happen.

One day, I saw a guy that lived on our street and he said, "Alright Ian, you're home a lot these days."

I said, "Yeah, the Navy kicked me out, I've got the same condition as Dad."

"Bloody hell," he replied, "you're a right bunch of cripples over there aren't you."

Just having to explain that the Navy had kicked me out to everyone who asked, made me feel like a failure. There's no way of dressing it up. The Navy didn't want me, I was not good enough for the Navy, I was not fit enough for the Navy. Failure, worthless, useless – oh and I've got a disability that no one understands either. On top of that, Dad thinks I'm a slacker because I haven't got myself a job cleaning windows or stacking shelves. I was at rock bottom. Every time that I explained my situation, I was reinforcing the message that I'd been rejected. It almost seemed like an act of self-flagellation but there was certainly no pleasure involved.

I was missing the Navy like mad. The banter, the camaraderie and the force's sense of black humour. I would spend my evenings hiding away in my bedroom, that way I didn't have to engage with anyone. There used to be a popular program on TV called "Soldier Soldier", it was quite good, and I'd watch it most weeks. I watched one particular episode that highlighted the bond between the platoon and the unique experiences that they shared. I found myself crying, it was everything that I had lost.

No matter how hard I tried, I was struggling to lift myself out of the gloom. It would be easy to have said, "come on, pull yourself together." I was trying but it was like I was walking in treacle. On the outside I was putting a brave face on things and trying to get on with life, but inside I was broken. One night I'd gone down to the local, Dad always went on a Wednesday, Friday and Sunday; I decided to join him for one before closing. I'd been talking to one of the locals, John McKnight, a great guy who was the father of one of Paul's ex-girlfriends, and a former policeman from Liverpool.

I'd been explaining that I was struggling to readjust to civilian life and John said he also found it tough when he left the police. I found it a really helpful conversation, and at last there was someone who could at least understand what I was feeling. Dad finished his pint and said, "If you're that screwed up, why don't you write a book, that's what other screwed up servicemen do." Once again, I couldn't believe my ears.

I eventually decided that I would like to use the experience that I had gained, working in the world of intelligence up in Scotland in my future career. I had really admired the linguists that we worked with, whose focus had changed from Russian at the end of the Cold War, to Serbo-Croat as the Balkan conflict erupted. I gave some thought to the geopolitical situation globally and what threats or problems would the intelligence services of the future need to be dealing with. Ideally, I'd have loved to have worked in Ireland but with my diagnosis, that really wasn't going to happen. I decided that I'd like to learn Spanish. The drug trafficking situation in South America was a constant issue and I had this pipe dream of working in a security role out in the Caribbean – if I could speak Spanish, then maybe I'd have a chance. The truth of the matter was that I had absolutely no idea what I wanted to do so I might as well spend my time educating myself in something I had an interest in.

Naturally, this went down like a fart in a spacesuit with Dad, His layabout son was going to become a layabout student. I think Dad's view on students was formed, having watched the *Young Ones* on the TV, so I didn't stand a chance really.

I applied to Durham University to study Spanish. I chose Durham because I knew there was a really good standard of cricket being played up there. They offered me a provisional place for their 1995 intake on the understanding that I completed an Access Course. I enrolled at Deeside College and started in September 1994.

It was around this time that I had a chance meeting with the girl who was later to become my wife. I was leaving a bar called the Potter's Wheel in Buckley when our paths literally crossed. I was walking out, and she was walking to the bar. I said, "You are the most beautiful girl in the world." The next night we bumped into each other again in a different bar.

I'd asked her out a couple of times, but she declined. Then on New Year's Eve 1994, she eventually said yes. I knew almost immediately that I wanted to marry Joanna. She was lovely, a student nurse who was training at Warrington

General Hospital. We dated for a couple of months, and then one night after we'd returned from a night out in Liverpool, she told me she wanted to end it. I was a bit miffed. to say the least. I certainly hadn't seen it coming.

I had a holiday booked over Easter to Barbados with my brother and a mate of ours. So, I resolved to put Joanna behind me and just have a good time on holiday, watch some cricket and drink some rum.

A couple of weeks after I returned, I saw Joanna again. She came over and explained that she'd had some time to think and wondered if we could get back together again. We're still together now, 26 years later, and married for 23 of them. It has been the best decision I ever made. She has been a rock and the love of my life. She has the blackest sense of humour of anyone that I met outside of the Navy, although only those very close to us get to see it. We laugh constantly and she has been the perfect mother to our children.

As our relationship developed, it was clear to me that being with Jo had become far more important to me than college and any future perfect job aspirations. Neither of us had much money, Jo had a minimal income as a student nurse, and I had the very small invalidity pension given to me by the Navy. We had enough to enjoy some nights out but nothing more than that. It was obvious to me that if we were going to make something of our relationship, then I needed to get a job.

For my first job outside of the Navy, I returned to what I knew best. I got a job with the MoD at an RAF Station, down the road from where we lived. It paid a pittance, and I was overqualified for the job, given my experience in the Navy, but I had to start somewhere. To all intents and purposes, I was starting again at the bottom. Everything that 12 months earlier I didn't want to contemplate. The job was awful and the prospects of promotion non-existent; I needed to find something else.

Mum worked for a firm of Surveyors and Estate Managers in Chester and was pretty sure that she could get me a job assisting her with the account management of some of the landowner's estates. Sure enough, I went for an interview with one of the partners and was offered a job. Slightly more money than what I was earning, and they'd cover some course fees, as I embarked on gaining some accountancy and bookkeeping qualifications.

I can't lie, working with Mum was a struggle. She knew her job inside out but would not be told by anyone that there might be a simpler way of doing things, or that she had made an error. I had taken on more accounts over the time that I had been there, my responsibilities had increased, but my salary never did. One day, I took the bull by the horns and went and had a chat with one of the partners. I explained that Jo and I were saving for a house and how much I had developed since I had begun working there. Would the partners consider giving me a pay rise?

Mum was mortified. She finished an hour earlier than I did, and by the time I got home, Dad had been fully appraised of my cheek. Apparently, I was lucky to have the job at all; how dare I embarrass my mother, who did I think I was? That was an awful evening, I'd had a reasonable conversation with the partner but I never got the chance to explain that before being reduced to feeling worthless again.

Next day, I was called into the office by the partner that I had spoken to the day before. They had agreed to give me a £2k-per-year pay rise. I didn't bother telling Mum or Dad. Mum would find out when she ran the payroll anyway. Whilst the pay rise was welcome, it was clear that I could not carry on working with Mum. The job wasn't stretching me, we clearly wound each other up the wrong way and I wasn't happy.

I'd been outside of the Navy for two years at this point. When I left, I could still jog, and walking wasn't an issue. I could climb stairs and walk up hills. By the end of 1996, I couldn't jog any longer or ride a bike. I'd tried to play cricket for my local club, but it was awful. It was nice to put whites on again, but I wasn't competitive and was compromising the team. I wasn't enjoying it so I stopped playing.

I'd been contacted by the MoD's newly established Gulf War Medical Survey. The government had reluctantly accepted that the number of medical complaints raised by people who had served in the Gulf warranted further investigation. Joanna accompanied me on two trips to London to take part in this survey which took place at the Central Middlesex Hospital.

I ended up being sat in front of an RAF Wing Commander (I think) who was in charge of the survey. He said he was pleased to inform me that my service in the Gulf had led to no major health issues. "However, we have this problem with your legs don't we, what are your thoughts?" I replied that I felt it was too coincidental that I was suffering with a neuro-muscular condition that was diagnosed 18 months after my return from the Gulf and having received the injections that I did.

He said the following, "I agree, it is very coincidental. But the problem that you have is proving that the injections were responsible. To do that. you would need to take the MoD to court and I don't think you can afford to do that. My advice to you is to walk out of here and get on with your life."

So I did.

Joanna had been wonderful for me,, she'd found me at my lowest and given me purpose and a new focus and direction in life at a time when I had nothing. We got engaged in May 1996 and bought our first house in October that year. By January 1997, I had a new job. I began working for Marks and Spencer Financial Services on the business park in Chester. I was delighted because I felt I'd found a job where I could work hard and hopefully advance myself. M&S were a good company and I knew people who worked there. For the first time since I'd left the Navy, I felt settled and secure.

We were the first of our group of friends to get married. Therefore, my stag do set the benchmark for all the lads that followed over the coming years. On a Friday afternoon in June 1997, 16 of us met at our village local and boarded a minibus to Manchester airport. Destination Amsterdam.

I can't go into the details of what went on, mainly because I can't remember much of it. It is sufficient to say that you learn a lot about your mates in a place like Amsterdam, and some of mine were feral.

The final indignity for me came just when I thought I'd got away with it. In the minibus back home from the airport on the Sunday evening, I was stripped naked, all except my boots. They wrapped me up like an Egyptian mummy in cling film and slipped a Liverpool shirt over my head. I was furious but there was no point fighting – because I couldn't.

As we entered the town centre in Buckley, a mile from home, the minibus stopped. I was bundled out and placed up against a lamp post. The offending football shirt was removed, leaving me stark bollock naked, using my hands to protect my modesty. They then got the cling film and wrapped it around me and the lamp post. They all got their cameras out and got a photo with me before boarding the minibus back to our local.

So there I was, naked and cold and unable to move. Then the pubs closed and people started leaving to make their way home. Two women were the first to approach me. They kindly unwrapped me from the lamp post.

I was able to waddle around the corner to the taxi office, which, by the time I got there, was full of pissed up locals, all needing a lift home. Needless to say, I provided everyone with a late-night laugh.

Jo and I married in July 1997. I'd managed to persuade her that we should delay our honeymoon until the following April, when England were playing in the West Indies; so straight after the wedding, we went down to Plymouth where we stayed at the home of a mate of mine from my Navy days. We had a lovely week and returned home to move into our new house.

In the weeks leading up to the wedding, and since returning back to work, I'd lost a considerable amount of weight. I was also permanently thirsty; it wasn't an ordinary thirst, it was raging. I was up and down to the toilet at work to drink water and up and down during the night to go to the fridge for a cold drink. I was preparing a litre bottle of tap water before I went to bed and putting it in the fridge. By the morning, it was empty. Joanna suspected that I was diabetic and that I should go to the doctor. I ignored her because I didn't want to believe it. Eventually, I took her advice and went to see the nurse at work and explained my symptoms. She did a quick blood test and diagnosed diabetes immediately. Three hours later, I was in a hospital bed and receiving insulin. Not for the first time, I was on a hospital bed wondering what on earth was going on. Joanna was really upset. At the time, she was working on the Renal Unit at Wrexham hospital; she was treating diabetics who had gone into renal failure, one of the side-effects of diabetes. She knew how serious the condition was, I was oblivious to it.

I was in hospital for a week and off work for a month whilst my blood sugar levels stabilised, and I got used to injecting myself with insulin 4 times a day and blood testing. This was a whole new world for me. Experiencing a hypo for the first time was very bizarre. Hypoglycaemia is when the levels of sugar in your blood drop so low that your brain starts to shut down non-essential systems in order to keep the essential ones functioning. Different people experience different symptoms and warning signs of hypo's, some people don't get warnings at all. Thankfully I do, I start feeling lightheaded, I break out in a sweat and just want to shut my eyes. A glass of coke or Lucozade and a sandwich usually brings my blood sugar levels up to a safe level, but I feel crap afterwards.

Managing diabetes is hard work, you have to find a balance between having enough carbohydrate to function but not too much to send your blood sugar sky high. Then you need to calculate how much insulin you need to take to compensate for your carbohydrate intake. Frankly, it's horrible. I've been fortunate, I've never been hospitalised as a result of a hypo and I've never experienced diabetic coma, but it is always there, like a monkey sitting on your shoulder watching everything you eat and drink.

I'd been at M&S for a couple of years when an opportunity was advertised to become a trainee manager. I applied and was offered the position. For the first time since I'd left the Navy, I felt as if I had a career that was providing me with opportunities should I work hard enough to take advantage of them.

Since leaving the Navy, my levels of physical activity had dropped considerably. My condition had started to deteriorate and things that I could do at the time when I left the Navy, I could no longer manage. I had not accepted that what I had was a disability, I didn't want to have a blue badge because I didn't want to be labelled. I could walk to the pub for a pint with my mates and I could go out with Jo without my limitations causing too much of a problem. I was struggling with stairs and hills at this stage and I'd noticed that my balance was starting to be affected. If we went shopping in Chester, for example, and it was crowded, I couldn't move quickly enough to get out of people's way. And if I got accidently knocked, then I would lose my balance and fall into someone else. Slowly but surely, the condition was starting to impact me in more and more ways.

I'd stopped going on big nights out either to Birkenhead, Liverpool or Chester. When Jo and I met, we'd go to the local nightclub, The Tivoli Ballroom, in Buckley. Now don't get the wrong idea about the Tiv, it's as close to being a ballroom as I was to running a marathon. But it was great, Friday and Saturday nights and Christmas and New Year, it was rocking. They had some great bands play there too, Oasis, Lightening Seeds and The Seahorses, to name a few. But for me, going out was becoming more and more precarious. My balance had worsened, I fell a lot and the natural reaction when you fall in a pub or a club is that you're drunk. I'd get really frustrated, having to explain to door-men that I had this problem with my legs and I'd hate being questioned about why I was using a disabled toilet when the Gents were either up or down stairs. The frustration was that people didn't know. At that point, I had no sticks or a wheelchair, just splints on my legs that people couldn't see. The anxiety of avoiding crowded places or going somewhere new was, and still is, almost as disabling as the condition itself. At the start of a night everybody says that they'll look after you and make sure that you're alright, but six pints later, nobody gives a toss. Why would they? They've worked hard all week and are enjoying a night out.

Genetic Counselling and Conor's Arrival

Jo and I had been married for three years in 2000 and inevitably we started talking about having a family. It just wasn't that simple though. We knew already that there was a 50% chance that a child of ours might inherit CMT. There was also the possibility that our children may have a birth defect due to the injections that I had been given in the Gulf; plenty of other servicemen had experienced this. CMT presents itself in different ways in different people, even within the same family. Therefore, our children could have it worse than me, not as bad as me or not have it at all.

It's the ultimate ethical dilemma. Knowing what we knew about my medical history, should we even have been thinking about bringing a child into the world? My view was that whether the child had CMT or not, I wouldn't want to deny anybody the life that I had up until that point. The highs outweighed the lows. Joanna countered that what if our child didn't have the strength of character that I had in dealing with the disability? I don't know if there is a right answer or not but we both decided that we wanted children and we would be there for them whatever happened.

We had been trying for a baby for just under a year and had been unsuccessful. The week that I had an appointment with the Dr to have some fertility tests done, we found out that my swimmers had done the job and she was indeed pregnant. Our first child was due in January 2001. We were ecstatic, for a couple of weeks at least. The next eight and a half months were hard work emotionally for us both and physically for Jo.

Because of my diagnosis of CMT and my service in the Gulf, we had to go for genetic counselling. During these sessions, the risks were laid out to us straight. We could have this test and that test, and we could abort if we wished. Given the amount of deliberation that we had already gone through, these sessions just messed with our heads even more. Abortion was out of the question. We'd made our decision and we intended to stick with it.

About eight weeks into the pregnancy, a blood test established that our baby was at 1/120 risk of having Down's Syndrome. Of all the things that we had considered and fretted about, Down's wasn't even a factor. Again, we were offered all sorts of tests to establish whether the baby had Down's or not, but some of them carried risk of miscarriage at worse odds than the risk of Down's. We decided to wait until the 20-week scan when they would be able to tell us for definite.

Jo really struggled with morning sickness right up until the 20-week scan. They confirmed that our baby didn't have Down's, and they asked if we would like to know the sex of our child. We both agreed and were delighted to be told that it was a boy. The rest of the pregnancy was uneventful up until the night when Jo went into labour, when our soon to be born son really put us through it.

We'd gone to the hospital late afternoon and Jo was settled into the maternity ward and hooked up to all these different monitors. So far so good. After a few hours, it was clear to me, as the observant bit-part husband, that the midwife was showing a little concern about something on the monitor. A doctor came in and they had a discussion which was not shared with me. Jo was on gas and air by this time and out of the game. They monitored the situation for 20 minutes and then the midwife pushed a button. All hell broke loose. It was clear to me that something was very wrong, but I didn't know whether there was a problem with the baby or my wife – nobody spoke. All of a sudden there were about 10 people in the room and within a minute, my wife had a form shoved in her face which she scribbled on and was rushed away, and I was left in the room on my own, not knowing what the hell was going on.

I was in pieces at this point. Obviously, there was an issue, but I didn't know what it was or who had the problem, Jo or our baby. I sat head in hands, wondering what on earth was happening to my wife when a cleaner walked into the room. "Alright lad," she said as she picked up discarded paper sheets and other medical waste from where my wife once lay. Now, I must have looked awful at this point, it must have been fairly obvious to the casual observer that I was not "alright". Neither was I in the mood for small talk. "Your Mrs OK?" she enquired. I was struggling to find a response with more than two syllables and without an ending of "off" when a nurse walked in wearing surgical gowns and said, "Would you like to meet your new son?"

As I held him, the nurse explained what had happened. Somehow, he had done a somersault in the womb and put a knot in the umbilical cord. As he headed south to make his entry, the knot got tighter and tighter and was cutting off his blood and oxygen supply. Thankfully, this was noticed by the nursing team and Jo was rushed off for an emergency caesarean. We had been fortunate that an anaesthetist was only five minutes away. If they had to wait any longer, we'd have lost him. The whole drama couldn't have lasted more than 10 or 15 minutes between the alarm being pressed and me holding our newborn. It was the longest 15 minutes of my life. Joanna, bless her, was out for the count but she was going to be sore when she came round. The thought of losing either of them was sickening and for that period of time when I didn't know what was happening, I was distraught and powerless and very isolated. I couldn't wait to see Joanna and show her our son but that would have to wait until the next day.

I drove home and poured a giant rum; my drink of choice after a dramatic life experience.

The bundle of joy that was handed to me that night is now 20 and 6'3" and it's fair to say I haven't stopped worrying about him from that day to this.

With Joanna needing to stay in hospital for several days to recover from the caesarean, I was back and forward to the hospital a couple of times a day so there wasn't an immediate opportunity to wet the baby's head. An opportunity did present itself, however, on the evening before the day I was due to bring Joanna and Conor home from hospital. I was looking forward to a good few beers and then a good night's sleep and getting to the hospital nice and early to bring my family home. It didn't quite happen like that.

I'd gone out with my brother, and my mate Alun. One drink led to about 10, a kebab and then somehow we got home – I can't remember how or at what time. I remember wanting to be up early as Jo's Dad was coming down to finish tiling our kitchen at 8 am the following morning. The alarm went off at 7 am. I felt awful, my head was banging. Then, *ughh what on earth was that smell? Oh no, hang on I'm wet, did I spill a drink?* The realisation soon set in. I was lying in bed, with my jeans still on and I'd wet the bed. This was disastrous. I'd never been that drunk in years. The throbbing pain in my head, the soaking wet jeans, sheet and mattress and that bloody awful smell told me it had been a pretty monumental evening. There was no time to try and remember the evening, I was on a countdown to a knock on the door from the father-in-law. I stripped myself, followed by the bed and got the offending items in the washing machine. All the bedroom windows were opened and the mattress was leant up against the radiator in a pretty poor attempt to get it dry for when Joanna got home. Windows wide open, beginning of February, nothing remotely suspicious about that.

My father-in-law, John, arrived bang on time to find me fresh as a daisy, at least on the outside, and industrious in the kitchen. The kettle was on and the washing machine was going, what a great son-in-law I was.

I was in no fit state to drive. I called Joanna in the hospital and advised that it would be early afternoon before I'd get to her. As John cracked on in the kitchen I felt an urgent need to fall asleep. Alun's girlfriend Suzanne came round thinking that Jo would be home with Conor. I had to explain what had happened and the predicament that I was in. She spent time using a hair dryer to dry the mattress. It was all hands to the pump.

I eventually picked Joanna and Conor up at about 4 pm. I'd been looking forward to this day for so long, it's a lifetime milestone bringing your newborn baby home for the first time. I had the hangover from hell, a baby crying and a very unhappy wife. That was before I told her about the damp mattress.

Disability Cricket

I'd not played any form of cricket since I stopped playing for my local club team just after I left the Navy. I really missed it. It wasn't just about missing playing but also the camaraderie and banter that goes with being part of a team sport.

One evening, just before my 30th birthday in May 2000, I saw an advert in our local paper where a guy was trying to recruit cricketers that had some form of disability. This sent me into a bit of a spin. I knew my legs weren't right but I never considered my condition a disability because I never believed that there was anything that I couldn't do. That said, I'd stopped playing cricket because my condition didn't allow me to compete on the same level as others. The distance that I could walk had reduced considerably and I couldn't run – but was it really a disability? That newspaper advert made me think more deeply about my condition than I had ever done.

I knew that if I replied to the advert, I would be accepting in my own mind that I had a disability, a weakness, a limitation – all things that as a bloke we don't like to accept. Was I ready for that level of acceptance, what would Joanna think, what would the lads think?? On the other hand, I recognised that if I didn't at least make an inquiry, then I would never know and an opportunity to fill a gap in my life would be missed. I still lived and thought like an able-bodied serviceman but my physical limitation brought me so many frustrations. Here was an opportunity where I might be able to compete against other people with similar conditions. Or, would their conditions be worse than mine? Would I be seen as a bit of a fraud? My mind raced at a million miles an hour that evening going over all of the ramifications of whatever I decided to do.

I never wanted to play on my limitations. Just thinking about being part of a disability sports team was messing with my head and my whole way of thinking. I was never interested in the Paralympics or any other disability sport. I just didn't associate my limitations with being a disability or making me eligible for disability sport. But then I thought, well hold on, my balance was poor, I couldn't run and I couldn't stay on my feet that long without needing to sit down due to fatigue. I'd left mainstream club cricket because I could no longer compete, and I didn't feel it was appropriate for me. So why not see what this guy has to say.

In the end, I just thought fuck it, I've got nothing to lose, and the next morning I picked up the paper and gave the number a call. I spoke to a gentleman called Paul Cartwright and we agreed to meet in Wrexham and discuss what was involved. It may sound hyperbole but that phone call with Paul Cartwright started a chain of events that changed my life, made me find myself again and gave me a purpose that had been missing, but above all else, it led to me being part of something again and got me back on a cricket field. For all of these things, I am forever grateful to Paul and the role that volunteers play in sport.

Paul was the coordinator for an organisation called the Welsh Association for Cricketers with a Disability (WACD). He explained that the WACD had just been backed by the Cricket Board of Wales (now Cricket Wales), and that they played in a national County Championship that had recently been formed and run by the British Association for Cricketers with Disabilities (BACD). I explained about my condition and my functional limitations and he confirmed straightaway that I would be eligible to play. He invited me to play for the Welsh Disabled team at an indoor tournament at Old Trafford the following weekend.

I had no idea what I was getting into at all, I hadn't met any of my new teammates but I turned up at Old Trafford and immediately thought that this was something that I wanted to be a part of. The County Championship season started some weeks later. I got to travel all over the country and played at some stunning cricket grounds. There was a lot of travel involved. From where I lived in North Wales it was a 4-hour drive to Cardiff for most home games.

That season, Wales reached the final of the BACD National County Championship largely through the efforts of an all-round cricketer called Paul Bennett. Paul lived locally to me and I remember him playing for Pontblyddyn CC when I was younger. Paul had a pronounced curvature in his spine but he was a great all-round cricketer and scored runs for fun at this level. We shared the car journeys with the other North Walians, Ian Crumplin, Paul Martin and Mike Hayes. Mike was a great lad; he was a wheelchair user and a former Paralympian who had competed at the Barcelona Games.

I took 5 for 1 in the Semi-final against Isle of Wight at Merthyr and we travelled to Trent Bridge for the final against Lancashire. To be fair, we were outplayed. Lancashire were a really strong side at the time. That first year really whetted my appetite for this form of the game. It also made me realise quite how bad my legs had become.

When I started playing again back in the May, we played our first Championship game against Yorkshire at Colwyn Bay. I walked out to bat on a grass wicket for the first time in six years. As soon as I took my guard, I realised that I just couldn't do things in the orthodox way anymore. I tried to play a drive and my left knee just collapsed under me and I was flat on the floor. My head, hands and eyes were telling me which stroke to play but my feet and legs just couldn't get me there – it was a horrible feeling. In the field, I had to be positioned close in because there was no way I could chase anything down to the boundary. I could no longer bowl anywhere near as well as I used to, I was now bowling flighted filth off one step just as Dad used to when I was a kid. It was clear after the first game that I had a decision to make. I either pack in altogether, satisfied that I'd had a go and it hadn't worked out, or I was gonna have to play in a wheelchair.

At that stage of my life and my journey with CMT, I wasn't sure about using a wheelchair. If I wasn't even sure that what I had counted as a disability, then using a wheelchair seemed a step too far and enhanced my fear of being thought of as some sort of fraud. If I hadn't rekindled my love for cricket, then using a chair wouldn't have even crossed my mind; but my desire to play was so strong, it became a bit of a no-brainer. I was clear in my mind that if I was going to carry on playing, then I would need to have access to a chair.

I needed to prepare myself for how other people would react to seeing me in a wheelchair. I'm not sure why this was a consideration for me but it was. I knew that people would look at me and now view me as disabled just because I was using a chair. I expected to get comments about why I used the chair sometimes but not all of the time. Such are the misconceptions about wheelchair use, people think that wheelchair users must be confined to them permanently. For the most part, I was still getting around OK but people never saw me struggling. Neighbours would only see me walking from the front door to the car. Work colleagues would only see me walking short distances and using the lifts rather than the stairs in the office. My mates would see me in the pub but there wasn't a lot of walking being done there either. In addition to all of my worries, be they warranted or not, people who also knew my dad would be asking, "Well why is Ian using a chair when his dad is clearly struggling more but not using one?"

Outside of the struggles that my dad had, I had never met anybody with a disability before. It was a new world to me. I hadn't accepted fully my own impairment at this stage. I was ignorant as to the needs of many disabled people and I never considered what anybody else needed outside of my own needs. I understood what I needed but not so much what others needed. I guess it is easy to become quite selfish in the situation that I was in. My limitations weren't obvious at that point, so I was never guaranteed of anybody else's consideration and other disabled people weren't guaranteed of mine. I think that it was during this period of my life when I began to understand the barriers to participation in sport that disabled people face.

All I needed was someone to understand my limitations and not try and fit me into a box – there were things I could do and things I couldn't. Paul Cartwright understood that in me and in the others that were in our collective. He didn't pretend to be the greatest cricket coach in the world, he worked with what he had and provided an opportunity that wouldn't have been there without him. I'm not sure you need too much more from a grassroots coach.

My desire to play meant that I had to get over these fears and worries. The decision to start using a wheelchair is probably the toughest decision people with similar conditions to myself need to make. It's a life changing decision that a person has probably wrestled with for many months, if not years. In many cases, the decision is taken after a particularly bad fall, or another serious incident when the use of a wheelchair has become essential. It marks the dawn of a new stage in the journey of life with a degenerative disability, a sign that things have gotten worse. In some, it can cause a grieving process as the reality of reduced mobility hits home. It can be damn hard.

I was lucky. Apart from my thoughts about how people would perceive me, I couldn't wait to get my wheelchair. The wheelchair was my passport to competing again in the sport that I loved. I didn't go through any of the anguish that some others do. It was very black and white for me; I either used the chair and got enjoyment from the sport or I didn't. At that stage, the wheelchair was only needed for me to play cricket. I didn't rely on it for everyday life.

In the space of a few months in 2000, my mindset and attitude had been completely turned around and cricket was the reason. I'd gone from living in a permanent state of denial and non-acceptance of my impairment to recognising it for what it was, accepting it and therefore accepting myself and who I was. Disability Cricket, through Paul Cartwright, had turned me from being someone trying to live a mainstream life, struggling quietly with a condition that I really didn't want to talk about into someone who accepted his limitations, found a way of dealing with them and who embraced the impairment for what it was and the opportunities that it now presented. People talk a lot about the power of sport, I am one of many who are living proof of it and all because a community-based volunteer put an advert in a paper.

Dad, of course, had his opinion. "You can't play cricket in a wheelchair... and anyway, what would you want to do that for, people will think you're disabled." I think this was around the time that I realised that seeking Dad's approval or support in anything that I did was going to be a fruitless pursuit.

Playing cricket from a wheelchair was difficult for me. It had to be done in order for me to participate, but it was like learning the game all over again. For a start, a good-length ball when batting orthodoxly becomes a short ball when you are in a wheelchair. A Yorker in an orthodox stance becomes a full toss, a short ball becomes an above-shoulder no ball. I needed to make an adjustment from judging length out of the bowler's hand and automatically deciding what shot I wanted to play because my new position required a completely different shot. It took me years to get anywhere near being any good at it. Essentially, I was having to retrain my brain to change responsive judgments and movements that it had developed over years. It was never going to happen overnight. It was hugely frustrating but at the same time, I was just loving being back involved in the game.

Throughout the early noughties, I worked hard on behalf of WACD. Paul had asked me to become the Secretary of the Association as we looked to formalise our relationship with the Cricket Board of Wales. After finishing work at M&S, I'd come home and spend my evenings on the computer writing letters to companies looking for sponsorship and support, or writing match reports for the local papers. I also produced programmes for our matches. I drew up our constitution and slowly but surely, we grew our committee structure and expanded the disability cricket program across Wales. We'd affiliated to the Federation of Disability Sport Wales and were recognised as being an effective and well-organised Association. For a while, we had a really strong committee which consisted of Lyn Samuel from Merthyr as Chairman, myself as Secretary, Paul as coordinator for North Wales, Simon Hickton, coordinator for Mid Wales and Peter Williams as coordinator for South Wales. Everybody played their part in helping the association run. We were relatively successful on the pitch too.

We reached the final of the National County Competition in 2000 and 2001, eventually winning the Final in 2002 against the Isle of Wight at Headingley.

I was loving my role, volunteering for the Association. I was a decent administrator and being able to fulfil this role in cricket and in an area that benefitted me directly by enabling disabled people to play cricket was brilliant. I started to organise an overseas tour to India for the WACD. I was in contact with Ajit Wadekar, a former Captain of India, who had set up an association for disabled cricketers over there. Ajit had sorted out the grounds and the accommodation. M&S said that they would provide the insurance cover, all our lads needed to do was fund their flights. I was in constant contact with Roger Fuggle, who was the ECB's Disability Consultant, so that they were up-to-date with the arrangements that I had made – this proved to be a smart move, as I shall explain later. Sadly, enthusiasm from my teammates was not forthcoming. None of them showed any interest in funding the flights themselves, or in finding sponsorship to cover the cost and I had to inform Ajit that we couldn't come.

My volunteering work in cricket was giving me far more satisfaction than my day job at Marks'. I built relationships with key people and organisations involved in disability sport, both locally and nationally, within Wales and further afield. As well as my role with WACD, I became vice-chairman of the BACD and began to work more closely with Roger Fuggle and learned more about the other disability cricket organisations that I had not come across before such as The England Cricket Association for the Deaf and British Blind Sport. I sat on the ECB's Disability Sub Group and was invited to join the Board of The Federation of Disability Sport Wales. My work in these voluntary capacities began to get noticed and I received a Service to Sport Award from my local Sports Council in 2002 and The Marks and Spencer Volunteer of the Year Award in 2003. I felt like I could make a difference in a world where my impairment didn't matter and where the business was delivering opportunities.

I made a decision that would be a huge gamble but I figured that those that don't roll the dice don't win the prize. Disability Inclusion was fast becoming a big issue in society and sport in particular. Roger Fuggle was a great bloke who I really enjoyed working with, but he was of an age where retirement wouldn't be too far away. If Roger retired, then ECB would need to make a choice; do they appoint another consultant or do they appoint someone full time to the disability role? If they were to recruit somebody full-time, what sort of person would they be looking for; what experience would be needed? I gave it a lot of thought and realised that at that moment in time, I didn't fit the bill. Wanting to do the job didn't equal being capable of doing the job. Something had to change.

In my day job, I was managing a team of great people who were having to phone Mrs Jones in Milton Keynes, who'd forgotten to make a minimum payment off her M&S card when she purchased a bra and knicker set and a Victoria sponge last month. It just wasn't doing it for me, so when the opportunity to join Disability Sport Wales came along, I had to take it. But before I could accept, I needed to run my thought process past Joanna who summarised my pitch to her like this:

"So, you want to quit a secure, well-paid job, with a great pension and staff discount to move to a job that is further away from where we live, with a £9k drop in salary so that you can gain the experience to enable you to apply for a job in the future that doesn't currently exist?"

"Yes, love. What do you think?" I replied.

It was a huge gamble. It depended on Roger eventually retiring and ECB deciding to replace him with a full-time employee. Even then, I would still have to get shortlisted and through an interview process. Many people would think I was mad but I thought I'd be mad not to give it my best shot – if it didn't come off, then it wouldn't be down to me not giving myself the best chance.

Besides, it had taken me a while to realise it, but call centres were the shop floors and production lines of the new millennium. No wonder I was losing the will to live. The madness of the 10 years since I left the Navy had seen me put myself into the environment that I vowed I never wanted to work in. Now I felt like I was taking control again and making a decision for the benefit of me and my physical and mental health. It was clearly not about money but about quality of life.

Joanna had been through all of this with me and given me strength when I was pretty much a broken man. She saw how much enjoyment I'd gained from being back involved in cricket and knew straightaway that she'd have a much happier husband if I was working in sport. I wish everyone around us had the same faith as she did.

Disability Sport Wales

I started a new chapter of my life when I joined the team at Disability Sport Wales in April 2004. DSW had an officer in each of 22 local authorities in Wales and I was the new development officer in Conwy. What a stunning county to work in. My patch covered from Abergele in the east and over to Penmachno in the west and south down towards Betws-y-Coed and took in some of Wales's most beautiful scenery. Driving to work on that first morning was liberating, straight down the A55 and along the North Wales coast. I'd drop down onto the coast road at Rhos on Sea and drive along the sea front up to the office on Dinerth Road. This was much more enjoyable that being stuck in the queue to get off the A55 in the other direction at Chester Business Park.

I was fortunate enough to become part of a well-established and high performing Sport Development team, led by a great man and former Welsh Guard in Jim Jones. Jim was the Principal Leisure Manager for the local authority, and he was rightly proud of the team that he led. I felt privileged to become a part of it, particularly as I had limited Sport Development knowledge at the time. I was able to learn from some really talented people, Paula Roberts, Caroline Jones and big Huw Roberts, or Mawr (Big in Welsh) as he was known.

Disability Sport Wales was a National Program that aimed to increase the amount of opportunities that disabled people had to access sport. We worked with local disability sports clubs, local schools and mainstream sports clubs to help them to make their offer more inclusive. I'd built up a great relationship with Michelle Daltry who was the program's National lead through my volunteering role within Welsh Disability Cricket and it was brilliant to be able to work full time in this development role with such a passionate and talented group of people.

I had my eyes opened to a whole new world. I first realised that there was an opportunity to earn a living through sport development whilst I was at M&S. I undertook a Level 1 cricket coaching course in Cheshire. I'd wanted to do it in Wales but the Cricket Development Manager (CDM) at the time wanted to deliver to a group of disabled people rather than have one disabled person on his existing course for mainstream coaches. I waited over a year from my first enquiry to get on a course in Wales, and I eventually called Cheshire Cricket Board to see if I could get on one of their courses. The CDM in Cheshire was a guy named Richard Newton, and he couldn't have been more encouraging to me. I explained that I was in a wheelchair and he was not put off in the least. "We'll make it work," he said. That was all I wanted to hear. The approach of two people in two different areas doing the same job couldn't have been more different. Trying to get on a coaching course in Wales made me feel different, awkward and not normal as a result of my impairment. In Cheshire, I was made to feel no different to anyone else.

I attended the course which took place over two weekends. I passed and I was now able to deliver coaching, albeit at the lower end of the pathway, but that was fine by me. I'd also been recommended to also take the Level 2 course as soon as I was ready.

Rich invited me to assist at some summer camps that Cheshire Cricket Board were running in the summer. M&S were really supportive of their employees working as volunteers in their local community so when I asked for the time off work to help on the summer camp at Chester Boughton Hall CC, the HR team were very happy to give me the time off to go and get involved. Less so my department colleagues and department manager, but I wasn't worrying about that when I spent two weeks out in the sun helping youngsters learn about the game that I loved. It was here that I started to understand the role of a Cricket or Sport Development team and it got me thinking that I'd missed my vocation in life. Why was I going through Groundhog Day, every day, in a call centre when these people were getting paid to deliver cricket coaching. I was in the wrong job.

18 months later, I'd left M&S and was working with DSW. Michelle really helped and supported me along with Jim and the rest of the guys at Conwy. My time there really expanded my knowledge and understanding of sport development and even more about disabilities other than my own. For example, I'd never worked with the visually impaired or the hearing impaired before. Neither was I a massive fan of other sports outside of cricket and football, but this role saw me working with Development officers from sports such as Golf, Rugby, Swimming and Netball, and also seeing officers from other Welsh government-sponsored participation programs such as Dragon Sport and 5 x 60

Officers. I started to understand more about Sports Governance and Policymaking at a national and a local level.

Around this time, I was invited to join the Board of the Federation of Disability Sport Wales (FDSW). FDSW are the Governing Body for Disability Sport in Wales and this role introduced me to how disability sport and the DSW program was funded and also the link between performance by disabled athletes at Global events made funding submissions to the Welsh Government more powerful and persuasive. Delivering talented, disabled athletes through the program was not only good for Wales' identity on the world stage, it was also good for the continuation of funding to support the grassroots. FDSW was led by a guy named Jon Morgan from Swansea and he is a great bloke. A more passionate advocate for disability sport I have yet to meet and I've never met anyone with a bad word to say about Jon.

If the reason I left M&S was to gain experience in the world of Sport Development, then it had proven to be a great decision. I still had no idea as to whether Roger was going to retire or what ECB might do if he did, but I was much happier as a person and loving my job. I continued my voluntary work in cricket. In late 2004, Roger approached me and asked if I would be interested in being the Team Manager for the first ever international tournament for Cricketers with a Learning Disability. This was a new project that had been borne out of a conversation that Roger had been involved in with Robyn Smith from Australia and Lizzie Vogel from South Africa. The tournament was to take place in the Western Cape in November 2005. It didn't take me too long to say yes to that particular offer.

I don't know why Roger approached me for the role. I'd like to think that he'd been impressed with my level of organisation and process when putting together the aborted Wales trip to India; the truth is, I didn't know, but I was hugely grateful for the opportunity and wasn't going to let anybody down. Roger was quick to put his management team together. He was going to be the Head of the England delegation, Pete Edmondson from Lancashire was our Tour Manager, I was the Team Manager, Bobby Denning from Lancashire was the Head Coach and Ian Powell from Yorkshire was Assistant Coach.

The next 12 months were taken up making preparations for the trip and ensuring that the players that we selected met the eligibility rules for international LD sport. I sorted out the eligibility process and liaised between the players and the UK governing body for LD Sport. I sorted the kit, the flights, the

90

visas. It was really full on. At that time, we were not given kit by ECB, so we used our own manufacturer. The sizes were a bit hit-and-miss and I spent loads of time receiving and sending kit back for alterations.

It was also around this time that some jealousies started to surface on the county scene. Physically disabled players were accusing Roger, myself and Pete Ed of being biased towards the players with Learning Disabilities. They saw that the LDs were getting an opportunity that PD players weren't. Then there were people questioning the appointments of myself, Pete and Bobby and Powelly. It really brought out the worst in people. They couldn't understand that we had been invited to send a team to this new tournament and that's what we were doing. The organisers stipulated that it was for cricketers with LD, so that is what we intended to provide. This explanation wasn't enough for some though. Some of the email messages I received around this time were embarrassing on behalf of the senders, such as the guy that said that LD players would not be able to appreciate the opportunity they were being given so therefore, it was a waste of money. The level of ignorance was unbelievable.

Nobody wanted to see an England Physical Disability tour more than I did but the reality was that the time wasn't right, other countries were not as developed as ours and there was no alignment to their national boards. Learning Disability had this structure in place where our team was supported by ECB; Cricket Australia and Cricket South Africa supported their LD teams too. We had a real opportunity to get international LD cricket off the ground.

2005 is remembered for England finally winning the Ashes back from Australia. I can remember where I was for the end of each match. The first Test at Lord's told a familiar tale, with Glenn McGrath giving Australia a pretty comprehensive victory. I was in work for that and there was no sense of the drama that was to come.

We had gone on holiday whilst the Edgbaston Test was on and we were down in Cornwall with friends in a static caravan. I remember staying in the caravan whilst Jo and our friends went off to play with kids. I was glued to the TV as Australia slowly but surely knocked the runs off. We only needed one wicket and Kasprowicz and Brett Lee were nudging and nurdling along. And then it happened. Kasprowicz gloved one to Geraint Jones and the campsite went mad. It appeared that I wasn't the only one watching the cricket. *Get In!* I was ecstatic. I couldn't believe what I'd just witnessed.

On the Sunday of the Trent Bridge test, I was playing cricket up at Llandudno. Those not on the field at the time were crammed into the tiny clubhouse, eyes glued to the TV, as Ashley Giles scored the runs that put England 2-1 up in the series. Another close call but we got over the line.

On the last day at Old Trafford, I took Mum and Conor. The scenes were unbelievable. Thousands were locked out as the gates were closed an hour before play started. I remember thinking that I was so glad we'd got up early to go. Conor had turned 4 earlier in the year and here he was taking in his first Test match and hopefully seeing England roaring to victory. The atmosphere as Steve Harmison roared in to deliver the first ball of the day was electric. Test match cricket at its best. Australia held out, Ponting played a fine innings and they were celebrating as if they'd won the Ashes. Michael Vaughan was right, momentum had changed.

Day 5 at The Oval and I was in the office in Colwyn Bay early. I couldn't concentrate, such was the excitement surrounding England potentially regaining the Ashes. The game was delicately poised. It was no use, I was never going to get any work done, I made my excuses to Jim and drove home. I got home in time to watch the session of play before lunch where Brett Lee was peppering KP with short stuff and KP kept despatching him into the crowd. Shane Warne dropped a dolly; it was compelling cricket and I couldn't take my eyes off it. I was so glad I'd left M&S as I'd never have been sat at home watching the cricket had I still been there. With this job, there was a lot of unsocial hours and weekend-working so I didn't feel too bad taking some time back to watch a moment of cricketing history unfold.

As we know, bad light stopped play and the umpires removed the bails and called time on the game. We'd regained the Ashes! Cue carnage around London and in particular at Downing Street and on the open top bus ride. It was described as the greatest series of all time and it's pretty difficult to argue with that.

That series epitomised what Test cricket is all about. The results of the match were the headline but just as thrilling were the daily sessions of play as the series was in the balance right the way through. There were several games within each game that contributed to the drama. Australia had McGrath and Warne, two of the best bowlers to ever grace the game and we had KP and Fred. Fred had the best series of his career in an England shirt and KP announced himself on the Test scene as if he had always been there, a pure entertainer. And to think there were some people that questioned his inclusion before the Lord's Test because he was replacing Graeme Thorpe. There's just nothing like the Ashes.

2005 saw many notable deliveries but in my world, none quite matched the arrival of Ciara Jane Martin on 21st February. Thankfully, this was a much more orthodox arrival without the drama that accompanied Conor's birth. The drama came a few days after we got Ciara home when Conor was practising his bowling in the front room. He delivered a ball that deviated off the lounge carpet and rose sharply to strike Ciara plum in the face, just where the visor should have been. She was about 7 days old but that didn't seem to concern her elder brother.

The year flew by and it was soon time to start packing for the tour to South Africa. Sorting some of the logistics took right up until the day of departure. Some of the kit alterations hadn't been sorted, and proving the impairment eligibility of some of the players was also very 11th hour.

I was elected as the Chairman of BACD and whilst I was happy to assume this responsibility, it made my position with WACD a bit of a problem. I didn't want to be seen to be still heavily involved with Wales whilst leading the national organisation. I didn't want anyone to think that there might be a conflict of interest so I stepped away from the Welsh setup.

Joanna had gone back to work early after Ciara's birth. The timing of my trip to South Africa wasn't ideal. I was leaving her to manage with a nine months old baby and a 4-year-old. We had known that this was going to be the case all along. It had never entered my head not to go and she never asked me not to travel. If I was going to land the job that I wanted, then these trips would become the norm and part of the role. Some people close to us didn't feel the same and made their feelings known privately. This didn't help. There was no issue between Jo and I so why should anyone else be unhappy on her behalf? I wasn't particularly happy at leaving my family but that is the nature of the job and I certainly hadn't worked the hours that I had only for someone else to gain the touring experience.

I don't think that I am alone in being very single-minded and determined in pursuit of something that I want. I couldn't allow emotion or sentiment to get in the way. I certainly wasn't going to be distracted by the views of people who didn't understand the role I was undertaking in supporting this group of players and staff or my longer-term aim. It was never going to be an easy ride touring with these lads and so it proved.

Departure day arrived. South Africa was an unbelievable experience for all of us involved. We left the UK not really knowing what we were going into but we couldn't have asked for a better experience; although it didn't get off to the best start.

We flew to Joburg and then needed to transfer to a different terminal to catch a connecting flight to Cape Town. On arrival in Cape Town, some of our bags were missing and other bags had been looted. First lesson learned – it doesn't matter how many times you tell the lads to lock their bags with padlocks, you still have to check. Lesson two – Always check what the lads have done with their cash. On arrival at the hotel, we had players with no toiletries and some with no cash – apparently "lost in transit".

The Australians won the tournament quite convincingly and we finished a disappointing third behind the hosts but we learnt so much about ourselves and the challenge of touring with young men with Learning Disabilities. The tournament was played with a standard cricket ball whereas all of our domestic disability cricket in England was being played with a softer, rubber ball called an incrediball. This was a huge change for our lads. The Aussies and South Africans had never used a softer ball so they were well used to the harder ball. I'm not saying that was a reason for the defeats, the reality was that we were well behind the other nations in terms of technical ability too.

One of the great things about touring is meeting likeminded people from the other nations. On that tour, I made lifelong friends with some of the Aussies in Paul Montgomery from Cricket Victoria and Robyn Smith who was the CEO of AUSRAPID, the Australian Inclusive Sport Body for those with Intellectual Impairment. On the South African side, I met Winston Stubbs, a tireless worker in the organisation of cricket for those with Intellectual Impairment and also Lizzie Vogel from SASA-II, the South African Sports Association for the Intellectually Impaired, both wonderful people.

One night, when we had a rest day the day after, we took the lads into Cape Town for a couple of hours to visit the V&A Waterfront. We had a nice evening and gathered back at the agreed meeting point for our transport back to our hotel. Before boarding the coach, I was met by Bobby Denning and our Physio Kate Peckham, who had been speaking to a couple of the Aussie management about staying on and having a few beers then catching a taxi back later. I wasn't up for it. I knew that my legs would not be good after a few drinks and I didn't want to become a burden on the others, I was happy to go back to the hotel to look after the lads.

Twenty minutes later, I was in a bar on the waterfront, drinking Springboks looking out over Table Mountain and the waterfront!! My arm was twisted good and proper and when Pete Ed offered to return to the hotel with the lads and Bobby said, "C'mon, we might not ever be in Cape Town again," there was only ever going to be one result… absolute carnage.

Me, Bobby, Kate and Powelly, our Assistant Coach, were joined by Monty and Rohan Larkin, the two Australian coaches. Rohan wasn't a drinker, but he is the funniest bloke sober I've ever met. A former first-class cricketer with Victoria, he had us all in stitches. Monty was also a funny bloke. The Aussies had christened us Poms with nicknames from the film Shrek. Bobby was Shrek (bit harsh on Shrek we thought), Kate was Princess Fiona and Powelly was Lord Farquad. I never got told what they'd called me or Pete Ed. We drank long into the night. Springboks are served in shot glasses and are made from Peppermint Liquor topped with Amarula Cream and they taste fantastic. Heaven knows how many we drank but Kate ended up in the loo being very poorly and by the time we came to leave, my legs had completely packed in.

Monty and Rohan held me up as we left the bar and fresh night air hit us which really didn't help. We'd travelled a few meters when Bobby found a discarded shopping trolley from the mall. There was only one place that I was going to end up. They lifted me into the trolley and I was abandoned to my fate. The ramped exit from the top floor of the Waterfront Mall led down to where the taxis were located on one of the quayside approach roads. Whoever was pushing the trolley, released it from the top. I gently gathered speed as the trolley bounced off one wall and gathered more speed as I descended another level into the next wall. I had no idea I had reached the bottom until I realised that I was hurtling like some kind of human missile on wheels towards the cars in the taxi rank. I can only imagine that it was Rohan that raced after me as the others wouldn't have been capable. Thankfully, I was stopped before I did any damage to myself or anybody else. We were creased up laughing. It sounds dangerous as I write about it now but it has been remembered by all of us as a monumental night out, certainly one of the best I ever had. In the cab home we got talking to the driver about crime and how dangerous it was, being a cabbie in Cape Town. He told us many stories of scrapes that he'd be in. "Do you need to carry a gun?" I asked, innocently.

"Yes," he replied, as he lifted a handgun from the driver's side door pocket, "just in case."

Outside of the cricket, the tour was memorable for many reasons. We travelled five hours inland from Cape Town, across the Klein Karoo to Oudtschoorn. The scenery was just stunning, there were zebras, antelope, Impala and Baboons, all wild. I remember having earphones, in listening to the Paul Simon Graceland album, such a great soundtrack to that journey and the villages and towns that we passed through. In Oudtschoorn, we visited an ostrich farm and I enjoyed ostrich steak for the first time. What a fantastic meat that is, so tender. I highly recommend it if you get chance. From there we went down to the coast and to George, where the cricket pitch had the flattest track I'd ever seen. We went to a reception hosted by the Mayor of George at the Town Hall. The South African team treated us to some of their traditional dance and singing songs from the struggles against apartheid – it was a wonderful thing to listen to. They then invited the England team to sing a response. The best we could come up with was Barmy Army.

We arrived home at the end of November, having learnt so much about ourselves, our players and touring with players with a Learning Disability. There were so many lessons learnt. We were also in no doubt about how far behind Australia and South Africa we were. The biggest obstacle to our development was our domestic use of the soft ball. This needed to change if we were going to be competitive in the next tournament in 2007 in England.

Jim Jones and Conwy Council were brilliant with me and my involvement with the national squad, which meant me spending over two weeks away from my day job. Both Jim and Michelle at Disability Sport Wales were really supportive and took the view that whatever experience I gained would be reinvested into my work in the community. It was also good for both the Sport Development Team in Conwy and Disability Sport Wales to have one of their officers working with a national squad. Sadly, it was harder work for some of our players to get time off work. I spent a lot of time writing letters to the employers of different players, pleading with them to give their employee time off work to play international sport.

In 2006 I was awarded recognition as Welsh Sports Administrator of the Year by the Welsh Sports Association. This meant a huge amount to me when you think of the number of people in Wales who play a part in delivering sporting opportunities. I was presented with the award in Cardiff at a meeting of the FDSW Board.

I was still loving life at Disability Sport Wales and working in and around Conwy. However, my inability to speak Welsh created one or two minor issues. I'd grown up in Wales most of my life, except for the period of time when I was away with the Navy, I'd lived in North-East Wales. I didn't identify as Welsh because I was born in Birkenhead and Welsh culture had not been part of my upbringing, particularly at home. Many of the people I grew up with were Welsh, but I don't recall any of them speaking the language. In fact, the only interaction that I had with Welsh speakers was with teachers in school. I didn't need the language to get by and achieve in life. Some of my mates are passionate Welshmen but do not speak the language. We reside in North-East Wales, literally five minutes down the road, Welsh is not on the national curriculum.

The further West you travel, the language is more prominent and it becomes first language for many. I was met on occasion with what I felt were extreme views regarding my stated nationality and my inability to speak Welsh. One Head Teacher would not let me into his school to work with the children in their SEN Unit because I could not speak Welsh. There was also a sense amongst some that even if you were Welsh but did not speak the language, you were somehow less Welsh than those that do. We are all a product of our upbringing, I certainly wasn't anti-Welsh, I had no need to be, but I lost respect for those who were clearly anti-English. My upbringing was shaped by Birkenhead, The Beatles, The Jam, Madness, Football and Ian Botham. I couldn't change that regardless of how successful I wanted to be in my job. Each to their own. Anyway, whilst I could have invested time learning the Welsh language, it would not be much help to me if I was to gain the job that I wanted. It was not going to make the difference. I wanted to be talking to BCCI and Cricket Australia about disability cricket – they wouldn't care if I could speak Welsh.

I'd come quite a way since I left M&S in 2004. I'd built a relationship with ECB, toured with the LD Squad, Chaired the BACD and gained experience in Community Sport Development. Roger and I had started to plan for the next Learning Disability Tri-Series which was to be held in England in 2007 and I'd formed relationships with key people in Australia and South Africa in relation to disability sport. In the summer of 2006, I undertook some voluntary work at ECB, working for their Head of Development, Pete Ackerley. I'd known Pete through my work on the ECB's disability sub-committee with Roger. Whilst I didn't do anything seismic during this voluntary role, it at least got my face known a bit more, and as Dad said years before, "If you do more than is expected of you, then, if nothing else, it leaves a favourable impression". I still had no idea whether my gamble would pay off, when would Roger decide to retire? What would ECB do if he did? All I knew was that I was doing as much as I could to position myself should a position present itself.

In 2004/5, Paul Cartwright and I made contact with the former South African legend Eddie Barlow. Eddie had retired to North Wales with his wife Cally, after he had suffered a stroke in Dhaka whilst Head Coach of Bangladesh. Eddie and Cally lived in Ruthin which is about 20 minutes from me and I got in touch to see if he would be interested in becoming a patron of the WACD. Paul and I went to his home to meet him. I couldn't believe it, here I was sat in the home of one of the game's greats. He still had his South African accent and his wife Cally could not have been more lovely and welcoming. Eddie was in a wheelchair; the stroke had affected him badly and it was such a shame to see such a sporting giant in this way. That said, he could not have been more encouraging to us and he later joined us at a training camp down in Brecon. Eddie used to put pads on and a South African helmet and stand at the end of the net giving tips and advice to our young disabled players. I was in awe of the guy but I'm not sure all of our lads knew who he was.

On New Year's Eve 2005, I received a call from Cally to say that Eddie had fallen the day before whilst in Jersey. Sadly, he had passed away. I was gutted, it was so sad. I was grateful that Cally had taken the time to call me, she didn't have to. I only knew him for a short time but what a bloke. I have a photo of him with, my son Conor on his knee, wearing that South African helmet. A lovely bloke.

I had arranged my volunteering stint for Pete Ackerley at Lord's to coincide with a memorial service for Eddie that took place at St John's Wood Church, just over the road from Lord's. Cally had invited me to attend but I couldn't figure out how I was going to manage it. It all worked out quite nicely in the end, and I took my place on a pew as some of the great and the good from the world of cricket entered the church to pay their respects. I took my leave at the end of the service and couldn't quite believe whose company I'd been in. At least one member of the congregation who didn't know me from Adam at the time, has gone on to become a respected and trusted colleague, David Graveney, who at the time was Chairman of the England selectors and who knew Eddie from his time at Gloucestershire.

The 2006 season was coming to a close and I played my last County game for Wales in a Semi-final defeat to Cheshire. Ironically, I played arguably my best ever innings in that defeat. One of my teammates said it was the best innings he'd ever seen from someone in a wheelchair. I'm not so sure about that and it didn't count for much anyway as we lost. I knew it was time for me to move on, I hadn't really been enjoying playing for Wales over the year and I was actually pleased for Cheshire who had reached their first County disability final. Some of their players had been in South Africa with me the previous winter and they'd developed into a really strong side whilst we had gone backward, mainly due to continuous infighting. I'd had enough of it. My work with WACD had opened new doors for me with BACD, and to a lesser degree, ECB, as I worked towards achieving my goals.

At the final a few weeks later at Leamington Spa CC, things started to slot into place. Roger took me to one side and explained that he'd told Pete Ackerley that the following season would be his last. Roger had made his call, I now needed to understand what ECB were going to do.

I was hopeful that there would be a full-time appointment. London had been awarded the 2012 Olympic and Paralympic Games the year before. Government were investing heavily in Sport and looking at all sports governing bodies, particularly the major ones, around what they were doing to support inclusion. It was September 2006, just over two years had passed since I made the decision to upskill and get the experience that I lacked, in order to replace Roger. The next few months would be interesting in more ways than one.

Disability Cricket reached a milestone in 2006 with the decision of BACD to introduce the hard ball into domestic disability cricket. After the LD Tri-Series in Cape Town, it became clear that if England were ever going to compete against South Africa and Australia, our players had to have exposure to hard-ball cricket. Pete Edmondson and I needed to get our fellow committee members to understand this and to accept a proposal to introduce a two-tiered competition that enabled those teams with more ability to play with the hard ball and those whose teams were more developmental to continue to play with the softer incrediball.

In those days, the BACD held their meetings at Walmley Cricket Club in Solihull, it was a pretty central location for people travelling from all over the country to attend the meeting. As Chairman, I made sure that the discussion around the introduction of a hard-ball competition was on the agenda. It was always going to be an interesting and lively discussion, and so it proved. Having witnessed what we did in South Africa, Pete Edmondson, Roger Fuggle and myself had an advantage over other members of the committee, some of whom were not convinced that a move to hard ball would work at all. Even so, some of the questions that were raised were bizarre. "What's a hard ball?" asked one.

"Disabled people can't use a hard ball," said another. These responses took me by surprise but we pushed on. The room was divided into those that could see the merit in at least providing the option of hard-ball cricket for those that wanted it and those who genuinely thought that it was unsafe for disabled people to play hard-ball cricket.

There had always been a hard core of players, mainly from the northern counties who wanted to use the hard ball. We had to consider the safety element because some of the players who played disability cricket were less able and less mobile than others, and so there was no way that we could do away with the incrediball competition which served these players well. However, there was no doubt that if we were ever going to compete at an international level in LD Cricket, and down the line in PD cricket, we had to have a hard-ball option.

We got the motion passed and later that year, we commenced a two-tier County Championship.

In Wales, it changed the dynamic of our group as the vast majority of our players now wanted to play hard ball cricket and it marginalised the less able members of our group. I remember being at one training camp at Christ College in Brecon where our squad was offered a choice of hard-ball net practice and incrediball net practice. It was never the intention to create elitism but I guess it was an inevitable consequence of the decision that had been taken – all of a sudden, some players who had never played with a hard ball in their lives thought that they would be seen as a better player if they went to the hard-ball net. I could see what was happening and made the conscious decision to opt for the incrediball net. I was the only one.

The strive for progress created different problems. There were those who thought it was the best move we could have made, and equally, there were those that lamented the change. It took a few years to settle down but I'm pleased to say that 14 years later the two-tier championship is thriving with more counties than ever taking part and most supplying a team in each tier.

Although I didn't know it, Christmas 2006 was to be my last working for Disability Sport Wales and Conwy Council. Our Christmas party that year was a lively affair at a hotel on the sea front at Llandudno. Huw Roberts and I decided to stay over, it wasn't a difficult decision. Clearly a significant amount of alcohol would be taken and I lived over 30 miles away so a taxi back would be a significant cost. Added to that, the Ashes was being played in Australia so there was the opportunity to stay up late, with a beer or two, and a fellow cricket badger in Huw. I don't remember what time I fell asleep but I do remember waking up very early and opening my eyes to find the Welsh Ginger Prince lying next to me – really not the image I needed to cure my hangover. I turned the TV on and put the kettle on just in time to watch Adam Gilchrist smash England all around the WACA whilst making the second fastest Test hundred of all time.

The backup plan, in case I didn't end up getting a job with the ECB, was to emigrate to Australia. We couldn't think of a better place to raise our children and as a specialist cancer nurse, Joanna's job was on their list of wanted specialist occupations at the time. By the end of the cricket season in 2007, we were three quarters of the way through the emigration process.

In August 2007, I decided to drop a speculative email to the BBC's Wanted Down Under program. The program offered the opportunity to Brits who were seeking to move to Australia or New Zealand to go and sample life Down Under and compare cost and standards of living. We got a very swift response to say thanks but no thanks because the BBC had already got enough families for the second series. *Not to worry*, I thought; it was worth a try.

A few weeks later, I was working away at my desk in Colwyn Bay when my phone rang. It was the BBC to say that they'd had a family drop out and would we be interested in stepping in? I didn't need asking twice and immediately confirmed that the Martins were in. We had about 4 weeks' notice. I immediately phoned Jo. I didn't know whether she had enough holidays but it was too late to worry about that, we weren't going to miss this opportunity. We were so excited.

We'd also booked to take the kids to Euro Disney during the first week in October so we had a busy few weeks planned.

Things were definitely coming to a head on many fronts. ECB had placed their advert online for a Full Time National Disability Cricket Manager. This is what I had been waiting the best part of four years for. I wrote and re-wrote my application a number of times before submitting it. I then just had to wait to see if I'd be shortlisted.

It was an agonising period of time. We had Disney and Australia to look forward to but then I knew that if I was fortunate enough to get the job, we wouldn't be emigrating anyway. How would the BBC feel about that?

Sure enough, I got invited to an interview at the National Cricket Performance Centre at Loughborough University on Tuesday, 3rd October. I was delighted. I had my opportunity to impress and my gamble taken four years earlier had started to pay off because I now had a chance to influence my future.

Then, as I went to enter the appointment in my diary, my heart sank a little. It dawned on me that I would be in Euro Disney with the family and some friends of ours on 3 October. *What was I going to do?* It was a no brainer for me – I had to attend that interview. I'd been building up to that day and this opportunity for a long, long time. Joanna understood, she always does when it comes to me and cricket. There were no cross words, and her support of me over the years has been unbelievable. I'm not sure how many others would be so understanding when it came to missing a family break, or even just part of one.

She would fly to Paris with the children and our friends on Monday and I would join them Tuesday evening. My interview was at 1 pm, if I was in there for an hour, I would leave Loughborough at 2 pm and drive to Liverpool airport in time to catch the 5 pm flight to Paris. Sorted.

It was the end of September and the next month was going to go some way to defining the next stage of our lives, one way or another. Whilst Joanna was thinking about how we were going to travel to Australia with a 7-year-old and a 2-year-old on a 24-hour flight via Hong Kong, all I could think of was my interview presentation. It became all-consuming.

The trip to Disney gave me a full day to rehearse my presentation before the interview itself. Joanna, Conor and Ciara left with our good friends Jenny and Jason Maxwell early on the Monday morning for Liverpool airport and the flight to Paris. I rehearsed and practised my delivery all day. By the time I went to bed that night, I could present it in my sleep. I knew that I had done all that I could in terms of preparation and I slept easy knowing that I could not have done anymore.

I woke early and ran through the presentation one more time. My bag was packed for Paris and I left the house just after nine, as planned. I'd arrive at Loughborough about 11-ish, with time to freshen up after the drive and do another run through. Well, at least that was the plan.

I arrived as expected and parked right outside the cricket centre. I had two hours to kill so decided to shut my eyes for 20 minutes following the drive before heading inside. Next thing I saw was Ackers striding over the metal bridge from the centre towards me. "Our 11 o'clock hasn't turned up, are you ready to go now?" he said.

I didn't hesitate, and 10 minutes later I was in front of the three people who would make or break my day. Pete Ackerley (Ackers) was ECB's Head of Development; Lesley Cook was ECB's Head of HR and Roger was the outgoing Disability Consultant.

An hour later, it was all over and I had time to drive back home and make some lunch before heading off to the airport to join the family in Paris.

I knew it had gone well, or at least I knew I'd done the best that I could. Whatever the outcome, I was comfortable with myself and my efforts.

Eight hours later, I was smashed in the back of a taxi heading from Paris Charles De Gaul airport to Euro Disney. Ackers had called me whilst I was sitting in the departure lounge at John Lennon airport to tell me I'd gotten the job. I was over the moon, ecstatic. Not sure how much I drank before the flight, but I know I polished off a bottle of EasyJet's finest Champers between take-off and landing. It was the best feeling I'd ever had; my gamble had paid off and I couldn't have been happier. And to top off a memorable trip to Paris, the following night I listened to Everton come from two goals behind against Metalist Kharkiv away in the Europa League. It was like the stars had aligned.

I was floating on air. Not even the queues or the extortionate prices at Euro Disney could bring me down. Getting up early with a hangover, to go for a breakfast with Mickey Mouse and my kids and what felt like the entire population of Paris and their kids, did, however, bring me back down to earth.

After I'd come back down to earth, there were some formalities that I needed to clear up. I needed to let the BBC know that whatever happens on our forthcoming visit to Oz, The Martins would not be emigrating to Australia. I also needed to advise my employers that I would be in for a week, away in Australia for two weeks and then off to join the ECB, starting on 5th November.

Physical Disability Cricket

When I first got involved in disability cricket in 2000, I was surprised to learn that we didn't have an England team. There were some really good players around in the County disability game who would all have been capable of playing club cricket to a decent standard. We were playing with a ball called an incrediball in the County Championship. It looked like a standard cricket ball except it was made of hard rubber and it had a white seam which quite often split if you hit it hard enough. The thinking was that it was safer for those with limited mobility to use this ball, mainly because it would do less damage if you were hit.

The use of the incrediball was a regular point of discussion, particularly amongst the better disabled players who longed to play, what they referred to as proper cricket, with a proper ball. I felt the same but also understood that if we did this, then we would definitely lose some players from the game – quite simply because they would be scared of the ball.

The discussion opened up all sorts of debate. There was an argument that said disabled cricket should be for disabled people, namely those who could not access the mainstream game. Those that were good enough to play with the hard ball didn't really need to be playing disability cricket and should go back to playing mainstream club cricket. I saw both sides of the argument but felt that if the game was to grow as a disability sport, we could be making changes that would see people leaving the game. So, for the first half of the 2000s, we ploughed on with the Incrediball. In the main, we were happy with the game. The Championship was run well and the standard was reasonable.

The game changer was the first ever International Cricket Series for people with Learning Disabilities. In late 2004 ECB, had been invited to send a team of cricketers with LD to a tournament against South Africa and Australia to take place in Western Province in November 2005. The tournament was to be run under the auspices of INAS, the world governing body for LD Sport and the approaches had been made to ECB, Cricket Australia and Cricket South Africa.

It was official and recognised by all bodies. We set about selecting a squad and a management team.

Throughout the summer of 2005, there was a lot of grumbling from physically disabled players about how the ECB had favoured LD players. I was regularly getting asked why LDs had an England squad and PDs didn't. The simple answer was that we'd been asked to send an LD team to a tournament, nothing more than that. There was a lot of jealousy about. There were some PD players openly saying that the LD players were rubbish and that ECB had discriminated against PD players. Some absolute rubbish being spoken.

The series came and went and England were well off the pace. We never won a game but learnt a hell of a lot. The biggest learning was that if we were ever going to compete against Australia and South Africa, we had to start playing hard-ball cricket. I had been the Team Manager for the LD Squad and Pete Edmondson from Lancashire had been the Tour Manager, we were both on the committee of the British Association for Cricketers with Disabilities (BACD) who delivered the County Championship on behalf of ECB. Pete Ed and I were both of the same mind that we had to introduce a hard-ball offer into the National County Championship. Pete drafted a paper proposing the change. As Chairman of BACD at the time, I made sure it got a space on the agenda of the next committee meeting.

What a meeting that was. The committee was made up of some lovely people, all devoting their time to ensuring we could manage and deliver cricket for the benefit of people with disabilities. Looking back on it now, I think that meeting was the start of the transformation of disability cricket from being run as a charitable program and recreational activity to growing into the multi-tiered and multi-formatted sport that we have today. Whether the Physically Disabled players at the time accepted it, it was the LD tour to South Africa that turned the dial.

Pete and I had a bit of a job on our hands to convince everybody that this was the right thing to do. I specifically remember two comments from committee members as we discussed the proposal.

"What is a hard ball?"

And, "It won't be safe, there'll be too many injuries."

I'm pleased to say that nearly 15 years on, I don't recall there being any significant injuries and what became the two-tier County Championship, went from strength to strength under the management of Richard Hill whose contribution to disability cricket has been immense. I was delighted to propose his recognition by the Queen and to see his subsequent receipt of an MBE for services to disability cricket.

As the LD squad continued to meet up and train as a squad in preparation for the next Tri-Series which was to be staged in England in 2007, the calls for an England Physical Disability squad got louder. We had some wonderful players available to us and they really should have had a platform upon which they could perform. Roger Fuggle, who was ECB's Disability Consultant at the time, arranged some showcase games that enabled us to get a squad together and play some matches.

One game was arranged at the Rosebowl in Southampton where two teams of Physical Disabled players were to play each other ahead of a Hampshire day/night fixture. Sadly, this game was rained off but not before we had our guys out on the outfield practicing. It was here that I saw one of the most remarkable catches I'd ever seen. Richard Whitehall, whom you may know now as the Paralympian "Marathon Man", played disability cricket for Nottinghamshire back in 2006. At the Rosebowl, he had taken his prosthetics off and was running on his stumps. He was taking high catches out on the boundary when his feeder must have sliced the hit and the ball went high to Richard's left. I watched as he ran around the boundary on his stumps and leapt a ridiculous height to pluck the ball out of the air. Richard Hill and I still talk about that catch today. Richard Whitehall, on the other hand, has gone on to achieve amazing things as a Paralympic athlete. A top man.

Another showcase game was staged at Bath CC. England LD against a Physical Disability XI, that was played before an England Women's International vs New Zealand. That was a great day, sun was out and we had a crowd in. I spoke to Charlotte Edwards and Sarah Taylor in later years and they both remembered this game and some of the amazing things that they saw.

It was quite clear that we had physically disabled players who deserved the opportunity to play on a bigger stage. By the time I replaced Roger at ECB in November 2007, those shouts were getting louder. We couldn't keep offering demonstration games. They were meaningless and also borderline freak show. Almost saying come and have a look at how well the guy with one arm can bat. It didn't sit right. But neither did creating an England squad for the sake of creating an England squad – they had nobody to play.

The Learning Disability model of teams being recognised and representing their National Boards was the way to go. This was the new way of delivering disability cricket. Blind and Deaf cricket, having been established much earlier, sat outside of the mainstream and I was determined that if we were going to get PD cricket off the ground, then it had to follow the LD model.

We were aware that physical disability cricket was being played in both India and Pakistan. The problem was that each country had multiple associations, all claiming to be the major body for PD cricket in each country. It made it impossible for their National Governing Bodies to control, particularly in India. Every year I would receive letters from each of half a dozen different associations, requesting that an England team goes to India to play them. Each time my reply would be the same, I needed a letter from BCCI to say which association was their recognised deliverer of cricket for people with physical disability. Each time I never heard anything back.

In 2010, I was in Sharjah with the England Blind Team who were playing a series against Pakistan. I was approached by Waqas Khan who was the President or Chairman of one of the Pakistani PD associations. We sat and talked about our will get PD Cricket played. I advised him of our position and I agreed to write to PCB to see if we could get to a position where they would affiliate with one association or another so that we could move things forward.

I wrote to PCB and told them everything I knew about PD Cricket in Pakistan. I advised that I wasn't prepared to have an England team play against an association that wasn't recognised by PCB as being representative of them. We maintained contact and PCB agreed to conduct an internal scrutiny of all organisations. This was a huge step forward. I'd managed to get an international board to take responsibility for disability cricket organisations who say that they represent them. Presumably at the end of this scrutiny exercise, PCB would affiliate with an organisation and make them the official body. Once that happened we, were all systems go for the first ever international series that was endorsed and recognised by two National Boards.

Sure enough, sometime in 2011, I received notification from PCB that the Pakistan Disabled Cricket Association had been recognised by PCB as the approved organisation for the delivery of cricket to people with Physical Disabilities. Now I could start having discussions with Pakistan about a series. This was also the green light that I needed to start setting up an England Physical Disability squad.

First of all, I needed a coach and a management team. We went through a recruitment campaign and did not find a suitable candidate through the process. I was recruiting with Gordon Lord, ECB's Head of Elite Coaching, and he recommended a guy he knew called Chris Ellison, a former pro at Yorkshire and who had completed his Level 4 Coaching course. I'd heard of Chris through work I'd done with his wife Annie. We'd worked together to provide cricket for people with mental health issues.

Ellers is one of life's good guys. So easy to get along with and we hit it off straight away. This squad was the first of its type that ECB had ever put together and I wanted it to be in good hands. I built a strong team around Chris, Will Kitchen as Assistant Coach, Neil Bradshaw as Team Manager and Kate Peckham as Physio. Will worked for ECB as a Coach Development Manager and was as opposite to Chris as you could possibly get. I hoped that they would rub off on each other but I'm not sure they did, as much as I'd wanted. Will is uber-confident, there's no ambiguity, you know what he is thinking. His dress sense, however... lets' just say is different. He will rub some up the wrong way, but life is never dull in his company. If there's an opportunity to take the piss out of something, Will finds it every time.

Bradders had been around disability cricket for a while, working with his partner Paula at Shropshire. He'd applied for the coach's role but he'll readily admit now that I made the correct call in not appointing him. However, what came through in his interview was that he would make an excellent logistics man, ideal for the Team Manager role. Bradders is an easy-going, diamond of a bloke. He's organised and detailed, exactly what I needed.

Finally, there was Kate Peckham our Physio. Kate had worked with me since the LD series in 2005 so I knew I was getting a great physio, and a female who could give as good as she got if the lads' banter got a bit much.

It was Autumn 2010 and time to get the players together and see what we had. I'd arranged the first get-together at ECB's performance centre at Loughborough. I'd invited David Graveney along. He knew as much about selecting England teams as anyone and was able to talk to the players about what is expected from England players and to wish them luck as they started on their international journey.

At this point, we were expecting the first international series vs Pakistan to be taking place in Dubai in 2012. Therefore, we had the 2011 season to look at the players and to decide on a smaller squad to work with, building up to the series.

The next load of grief I took came, not unsurprisingly, from the players that weren't selected to come and train with this provisional national squad. I got it all and from some unexpected places too. Apparently, I picked my mates for the management team. I had left out players who had played disability cricket for years and "deserved" to be in the England squad. One player told me that he accepted that he was too old to be in the squad but he should at least have been given the position of manager.

A couple of years earlier, we'd run what we termed a series of "Performance Weekends", specifically for those physically disabled players who were crying out for international cricket. We ran the weekends in the same way that we ran the national squad camps. Plenty of cricket and fitness drills during the day but the players were left to their own devices in the evening. However, they were given the message that recuperation and preparation for the next day were all part of the "Performance" environment.

It became clear the following morning that we'd got the wrong group. Some, not all, had massive hangovers. It was clear that a group had been out on the lash around Loughborough. These guys just didn't get it, at all. On another weekend nearer to Christmas one year, one of the invited players turned up at Loughborough, dressed as either an Oompa–Loompa, or one of the seven dwarfs after appearing in Panto the night before. He then got pissed off that people were laughing at him. You couldn't make this stuff up.

I was trying to establish some credibility for Disability Cricket within ECB and felt that some of the PD players at these camps just didn't give a toss. They didn't have the same vision or belief that I had about what a national squad should look like. You get one opportunity to make a first impression and I wasn't sure we were getting it right.

Sure enough, it was these players now giving me grief because they hadn't been selected for our first proper squad camps. It was so frustrating that these older players could not accept their time had been gone. The game was moving on and it was time for a new generation of players to come through.

The whole jobs for the boys thing was also just rubbish. I kept telling people that to become one of the boys in the first place, you have to work bloody hard and be in the game for what you can give to others and not take for yourself. There was a sense of entitlement amongst some that was just never going to work in the environment that I wanted to create. All of the people who were criticising me had been crying out for an England PD squad for years, yet now it was here and they weren't in it, they couldn't find it in themselves to support – much easier to criticise from the outside.

We had independent coaches, guys that had no experience of disability at all and therefore none of the nepotistic baggage that had hung around the game for years. There were players who had been living off the fact that they'd scored hundreds in the county disabled game – which was impressive until you realised that some of the opposition bowlers were bowling from wheelchairs or could barely walk. This is what had to change. The problem was, at that point in time, the County game was our only pool of players. I suspected that the players who were really going to make a difference were playing club cricket and not disability cricket.

The only selection criteria for an England squad is that the player is eligible in terms of nationality and the type of disability AND he is good enough to be in the squad.

There's nothing more to it.

I was receiving emails saying that certain people shouldn't be in the squad because they don't play in Disability County championship. Whilst I could understand the sentiment, it's the same as saying David Beckham couldn't play for England because he was playing for Real Madrid. There were players with eligible disabilities that were playing club cricket who did not want to play County Disability cricket for one or both of two reasons: 1) their club cricket was a higher standard of cricket 2) to play disability cricket as well would mean playing two games per weekend which they did not want to do.

Disabled players wanted an England team and at least we'd delivered one that would be run as close to the way that other England teams were run as we could get it.

I'd started discussions with Amir Uddin Ansari of the Pakistan Disabled Cricket Association in early 2011 about the possibility of Pakistan playing England at a point in the future. Amir was very keen for England to travel to Pakistan but sadly we could not do that because of the security situation over there. I advised him that it needed to be staged in the UAE if we were to do it at all. This was agreed and we started to look at potential dates towards the back end of 2012.

In August 2011, our Physical Disability side played a fixture against an Army XI at Bourneville CC in Birmingham, a lovely ground by the Chocolate factory. There was a bit of profile about the fixture with local TV, radio and several important ECB figures were also in attendance; Giles Clark, our Chairman, Dennis Amis, a Board Member and David Collier, our CEO to name a few. It had just been announced that the England Men's Team would be playing Pakistan in the UAE in March/April 2012 and it struck me that it would brilliant if we could use the profile of that series to launch the first ever Physical Disability internationals. All teams would be using the ICC Academy as a base, the mainstream media would be there en mass to cover the Men's series – it seemed to good an opportunity to miss. Thankfully, David Collier agreed. It didn't need much of a conversation, I picked my moment to suggest it to him and he agreed straight away. I was delighted and went to find Ellers to share the news.

He thought he still had just over a year to prepare his team for international competition and was a bit taken aback to realise he now only had about six winter months. All of a sudden, things were very real. I wouldn't allow myself to believe I'd instigated international PD Cricket until such time as we were in Dubai, watching the first ball being bowled, but this was a major step in the right direction. I knew that the Pakistanis would be ready to play at an earlier date and Amir's confirmation was soon received. We were on.

The months soon passed. Ellers, Will and Bradders set about selecting the squad and checking availability to tour. I ordered the kit and got the flights and accommodation sorted. Kit delivery never ceased to amaze me. We would supply our required items, quantities and sizes. Invariably, what we received bore little resemblance to what was ordered. There were different reasons for this but in the main it was because disability tours with any of our squads were late to be confirmed so when the kit orders were submitted for the season, no disability provision was made. Therefore, we ended up having to use any surplus stock that was left in the warehouses.

For this first PD tour, I was keen that the lads looked the part. It was important from an image perspective the disability squad looked the same as the senior squad – we were all "One England" after all. There were going to be plenty of photo opportunities and it wouldn't look good if the disability squad looked a distant poor in relation to the seniors in terms of kit.

When our kit arrived, there were items missing. No shorts had been provided and I seem to remember only two playing shirts. This was crazy. The lads were going to the UAE and likely to be training and playing in very high temperatures, so to not have any shorts was really disappointing. Bradders conducted an audit of which players were missing which items of kit and I took it back to the England Team's administrator at Lord's. Rob Johnson was the man at the time, he's a great bloke but I reckon he used to dread me approaching his desk when he was in that role. Every time there was a tour, there would be a problem with the kit.

I explained that we couldn't be sending an England team to the UAE without shorts. He agreed but he'd been advised by our kit supplier at the time that there were no ECB branded shorts in stock. But we still need shorts, what were we to do? Rob brought his boss in to discuss the issue. I got short change out of her.

"Your team have each been given a kit bag with over £400 worth of free kit in it. They should be grateful for what they have."

I was speechless. It was immediately apparent that not everyone in our organisation was bought into equality of opportunity or the need to offer a playing pathway to different sectors of our society. It seemed our lead licensing manager wasn't bothered what the disability squad looked like.

A week or so later, our kit supplier sent a box full of branded shorts, they weren't the official ECB shorts but at least the boys would look uniform and not like a village outfit. They also sent a box of hoodies by way of compensation which was very good of them.

These little battles became frustrating over the years. Although, to be fair, the types of battles I had to fight were different year on year which I guess is a sign of progress. Every now and again over a beer, Richard, Bradders and I will reminisce about the arguments and frustrations that we had back in 2006/7 and how different they were to the battles we have now. It's a sign of how far the disabled game has come.

One more headache to deal with before our eventual departure. Our last training camp, the weekend before we flew, was held at the National Cricket Performance Centre at Loughborough. Kate, our Physio, pulled me to one side and informed me that she was pregnant and that her Dr had advised her not to fly. Panic Stations – where on earth was I going to find a physio at such short notice? Step forward Fran Clarkson. Fran had worked with our Blind Team for four years and was my first port of call. Thankfully, she was able to arrange her time off from her NHS job to be able to make the trip with us. Fran is a great girl and a wonderful physio who is currently first team physio at Derbyshire CCC.

A few days later, we all assembled at the Marriott Hotel in Birmingham City Centre. Fran arrived and met the guys for the first time. I'd arranged for the Warwickshire and former England player Darren Maddy to come and talk to the lads before they departed. He was really giving of his time and spent a couple of hours with us sharing experiences and wishing us luck.

Once out in Dubai, we settled into the hotel and familiarised ourselves with our environment. The facilities at the ICC Academy at Sport City are second to none. What a place to train and then play cricket. We were there for two weeks and played 3 ODIs and 3 T20s. As the first ball was bowled in the first game, Bradders leant over to me and said, "Are you proud? You should be."

We lost both series 2-1. There were lots of lessons learned. The Pakistanis were street fighters, hard men who never knew when they were beaten. There's a point in every game of cricket where the game is in the balance and it can go either way – depending on scores and run rate, that critical point comes at a different stage of the second innings. Too often, we lost the battle when we could have gone on to win.

The series was memorable for reasons other than it being the first ever International Series between two physically disabled sides.

We spent an hour or so, netting with members of the England team who came down to the Academy whilst we were there. Callum Flynn was in the nets and had Stuart Broad and some others bowling at him. Flynny creamed his first delivery from Broad through backward point… I'm not sure he saw Broad's next delivery to him. The England lads were great; really good company. A couple of days later, the Pakistan team came in and Amir introduced me to Misbah ul Haq, Shahid Afridi and Younis Khan. They were all interested in our cricket and how it was developing.

For me, the biggest benefit that came out of this tour was the time that I was able to spend with Hugh Morris. Hugh, at the time, was the Managing Director of England Cricket and we had been talking for a while about how the England Disability Squads should probably fall under his remit. We spent an hour or so watching one of the disability matches and Hugh was really impressed with the standard of the cricket that was being played. It convinced him, I think, that we should be managed by him. I was made up because this would lead to more credibility for the disabled game and access to a higher level of Sports Science provision for the program. A short time after we returned home, I moved to be line managed by Hugh. Hugh is one of best, a really genuine man. I was gutted a year or so later when he called me and said that he was leaving ECB to return to Glamorgan.

Another advantage of being in Dubai at the same time as the England men's team was the fact that the media circus that follows them around was in town too. This allowed us to get some exposure through the mainstream media. Me, Ellers and Jimmy Williams, our Captain, did a slot on TMS with Simon Mann during the interval of an ODI between England and Pakistan. I did interviews with ESPN Cricinfo with George Dobell and Sky Cricket with Tim Abraham. I did an interview on live TV in Dubai on their news channel to promote the series. Before leaving the hotel, I walked through reception in a pair of mustard-coloured chinos and a nice linen shirt. Big Mistake. I'd forgotten that looking smart in front of Will Kitchen just made you a target. Well, to be fair, just being around him made you fair game for some sort of abuse. "Where are you going dressed like that?" he enquired.

"Off to the TV station to do an interview," I replied.

"An interview for what – to be their new testcard?" When I returned, my trousers had been given the nickname of Martin's Mustard Bumming Pants, no need to tell you who dreamt that up. Just in case there was any chance of me getting above myself or pleased at what I'd achieved, Dad told me I looked fat on Sky. So I went to bed that evening feeling fat and having shit threads. Another day in paradise.

Senior figures from ICC spent time watching our games. All were impressed. George Dobell interviewed Haroon Lorgat who was ICC CEO at the time who said that disability cricket should be supported and recognised going forward.

I'd done a number of tours by this time and learnt that no tour is without its headaches, whether it's allegations of cheating, media stories or trying to transport overweight baggage from one end of India to another. This tour was no different.

We had a rest day between the ODI and T20 series. That evening I'd invited our management team to my room for a beer at 8 pm. Slowly but surely, everyone trooped in, Will, Bradders, Richard, Fran and… where was Ellers? We gave him five minutes before opening our first beer. Next thing, there's a knock on my door. Ellers looked like he'd seen a ghost. There'd been an incident, it was serious.

Some of the players had been congregated in the hotel reception following our team meeting. They were just passing time, checking their phones and social

114

media etc. Matty Askin noticed that posts were being made on a player's Facebook account but the player concerned (let's call him Player A) was stood next to him talking to another player, and therefore, not on Facebook. The posts were pretty explicit and insulting and clearly whoever was posting them was going to embarrass Player A, whose account it was. At that moment in time the posts were live and Player A was being followed by a number of the Pakistan players who may well have been particularly insulted by some of the content now live on Player A's Facebook.

I had literally taken one swig of beer but it was clear that we needed to deal with things quickly. Will and I talked to Player A who, by this time, had quickly logged onto to his Facebook account and deleted the offensive content. It turned out that earlier in the day, Player A had borrowed the laptop of another player (Player B) to talk to his family back home via Facebook. Unfortunately, he never logged out properly. So when Player B got back to his room that evening and opened up his laptop, he was straight into Player A's Facebook account.

Player B was an introvert. A really nice guy and an exceptional cricketer a few years earlier. When we interviewed him, he admitted what he'd done straight away. He said he'd felt isolated within the group and felt he was struggling to fit in and he thought that what he'd done would be seen as funny and make him better accepted within the squad. I couldn't believe what I was hearing. He'd made a huge error of judgement that we would be very lucky if we got away with. We'd estimated that the posts were live for about six or seven minutes before Player A deleted them but who knows who had seen them in that time. I can't print here exactly what was said but it is sufficient to say that I was seriously worried that if any of the Pakistani team or management had seen them, or worse still, any UAE authorities, we'd have had a major incident on our hands and Player B's liberty may have been at risk.

I decided quickly that it would be for the best that we got Player B out of the country ASAP. There were two reasons for this. Firstly, he'd put the tour in jeopardy and put us in a situation that could have escalated way out of control. It was a huge error of judgement on his part. Secondly, there was no way that he could now integrate himself back into the group after doing that to one of his teammates. Player A was rightly livid about what had happened.

I spoke to our travel agent back in the UK and got Player B on the next plane out of Dubai and back home. I was pleased with how quickly we dealt with it and no one outside of our group knew anything had happened at all.

Well, that was until the next day when Player B's parents turned up at the Academy to watch our next game. I saw them walking over and had to go over and introduce myself and explain that their son had just landed back in the UK following a serious breach of our code of conduct. What a nightmare.

Some months later, Player B called me and apologised for what had happened. He'd had time to reflect and he realised what a misjudgement he'd made and what the consequences could have been for him and for us. Despite his momentary brain fade, in Dubai I still liked the guy. He was decent enough to make contact and apologise and I still remembered what a cricketer he was. Such a shame.

Two years later, we travelled to Dubai again to play Pakistan. Different squad, same results. We just couldn't get over the line. Ellers left after that series. I think he and I both knew that the group needed a new direction. He had taken them as far as he could. I admire him as a bloke, a really honest and solid guy. He runs a successful coaching business and at the time his family was expanding – it just felt like the right time to part company. We cross paths from time to time and it's always good to catch up with him.

Our new head coach was Qasim Ali. Qas was the lead coach at the Indoor Centre at Old Trafford and had been Ellers' assistant on the 2014 tour to Dubai. Will Kitchen had moved out to Dubai and was now Head of the ICC Academy, so there had been quite a bit of change.

2014 became a bit of watershed year for Physical Disability Cricket. I was contacted by the British High Commission in Dhaka, Bangladesh. They had been approached for help by the International Committee for the Red Cross (ICRC) who wanted to use cricket as a tool for rehabilitating people with physical disability back into society. They'd been made aware that ECB led the way with disability in cricket, and as such, requested our help via the BHC in Dhaka.

Several weeks later, in November 2014, Qas and I were flying to Dhaka to talk to Cricket Coaches about how to work with Physically Disabled people. It was an amazing trip. We were met by Emily Summers from the BHC and by Gerd Van De Velde from the ICRC. Gerd was Belgian and had no idea about cricket but he recognised that cricket broke down social barriers in Bangladesh in a way that other interventions could not. We spent five days there, we met everyone from disabled youngsters, cricket board officials, the British High Commissioner and Bangladesh Government ministers. The enthusiasm and hospitality with which we were met was overwhelming.

Although I'd seen high levels of poverty before in some areas of India, Dhaka was on a different level. I found it difficult not to appear really shocked by it. The other thing that amazed me was the traffic, the roads were just carnage. It was like the Wild West. Literally anything goes, there are no rules. Four or five people on the back of mopeds, rickshaws, tuk-tuks, buses that look like they take part in demolition derbies, cattle, cyclists, pedestrians – you name it, it's coming at you from all directions. On the plus side, you're never on the wrong side of the road. Qas and I were chauffeured around in a big Toyota belonging to ICRC, this thing was like a tank and claimed right of way wherever we went. Our driver was amazing. We believed that if you could drive in Dhaka without crashing or killing anyone, you can drive anywhere in the world. If a Brit was to take to the road in Dhaka, we would cause carnage. We'd be trying to drive to our rules and it would cause a whole new level of mayhem. Yet there's no road rage, no furious fist shaking and I'm guessing no insurance.

The outcome of our visit was the establishment of a structured disability cricket setup in Dhaka. Over 700 players. Soon after, there followed an invitation to what became the first World Series Physical Disability Cricket Tournament, organised by the ICRC and to be held in Bangladesh. Qas and I had sold a vision, ICRC and Gerd Van De Velde made it happen. Disappointingly, and despite previous promises and statements, ICC did nothing.

In three years, we'd gone from no PD international cricket whatsoever to our first World Series. ICRC undertook a review of the different associations in India to understand which of them was the most reliable and well organised. BCCI, the cricket governing body in India, had refused to get involved. I'd explained to Gerd that as soon as you invite one organisation in India, you will immediately upset the others. My preference at that point would have been to have not invited India *unless* a full scrutiny process was undertaken, and a preferred organisation was identified. To be fair to ICRC, that's exactly what they did. The All India Cricket Association for the Physically Challenged was recognised by ICRC as being the best organised association for disabled cricket in India. AICAPC was established by former India Captain Ajit Wadekar and I'd known of their existence for years, so it was no surprise to me that they had been chosen.

In one year, an international aid agency, supported by myself, had done more for physically disabled cricketers than the worlds cricket authorities had ever done. It was embarrassing, whilst I could stand tall and talk about what ECB was doing – there was not a lot else going on. ICRC recognised this and repeatedly said that organising cricket tournaments was not their remit.

After the World Series in 2015, which England won, there was then a demand by the Asian countries for more international cricket. Once again, Bangladesh stepped forward. However, there was a terrorist attack in Dhaka early in 2016 which immediately cast doubt on whether a tournament would go ahead.

Eventually, ourselves, Pakistan and Bangladesh took part in a Tri-Series in Dubai in September 2016 which was won by Pakistan who got their revenge after losing to us in the World Series final in Bangladesh 12 months earlier.

2015/16 was an amazing year for England Disability Cricket. In March 2015, our Learning Disability Squad won an Ashes Series in Melbourne. In September, the Physical Disability Team won their World Series in Bangladesh and in January 2016 the Blind Team regained the Blind Ashes on Australia Day in Adelaide. It was an awesome run and I was so proud of everyone, of the players and staff who contributed to such an achievement.

PD cricket had come so far. Until we had won the first World Series in Bangladesh, I'd never given much thought to how far we'd come. On reflection, I'm unsure whether I'm more proud of the playing of the first game in Dubai or the first game at the 1st World Series in Dhaka. England were beaten in that game by Bangladesh, a team that never existed six months earlier and only existed because of the input of myself and Qas Ali supporting Gerd at ICRC. I'd had influence in Pakistan and Bangladesh in getting PD cricket up and running and recognised; that, to me at least, this was something to be proud of.

In recognition of my work, I was invited to address an ICRC conference in Geneva in November 2015. I was on a panel with others who used sport to break down barriers. Quite an amazing place Geneva, and the ICRC Head Office was also pretty impressive. Bit expensive though if I remember correctly but then I guess most tax havens are.

Living with Disability

I have found that it is the attitude of others towards disability that has hindered me more than my loss function itself. I'm not for a minute going to say that life wasn't easier before my strength deteriorated but I don't think that my life is hard now, it is just different. In fact, my disability has provided me with a different set of choices than I would otherwise have had. I have travelled down a different road and been able to open different doors because of it.

The vast majority of people when they see someone struggling will offer some assistance. Dad hated this. Partly because most people are unaware of how to handle a person with the type of weaknesses we have. We need to find a point of equilibrium between support and balance – too much one way or the other and we are down. Generally, people are well intentioned, but I know from my own experience that sometimes I'd rather struggle in my own way, knowing that I will achieve what I want to, rather than have to instruct someone in how to assist me.

What I've learnt about this disease is that you don't have ultimate control over its progression or its effect. You can do what you can to mitigate the deterioration, but I feel as if I'm forever trying to find the balance between fighting it vs accepting it vs maintaining dignity. Dad didn't seem to bother with any of that, his approach has been more, to deny it, then stop doing what you enjoy when it gets too much.

Dad has been remarkable and unthinkable in equal measure. His resilience towards and resolute denial of his disability has no doubt got him through some tough times. Living with disability is not easy. His goal of remaining in work to put bread on the table for his family is testament to his values and his work ethic. However, his refusal to recognise his limitations became a burden and also a danger to himself, my mum and his friends.

Who is to say one approach is better than the other?

All I know is that I couldn't function in my job, or indeed my life, if I took my dad's approach. The more I think about it, I think it is a generational thing.

In my experience, people of my parents' age are much less comfortable with disability.

It never ceases to amaze me, the attitude that some people have towards the disabled. There are some who think we should be grateful for any opportunity that we are given. There have been times when I have felt like a member of some sort of underclass purely because I am using a wheelchair. I've been pushed around airports and duty-free staff have discussed my purchase and payment method with the assistant who is pushing me, rather than with me, whose money they are taking.

I have no scientific evidence of this, but I think that there are different levels of respect afforded to different people with a disability in our society. Let me explain.

Ex-servicemen, who have returned from battle with life-changing injuries, are rightly afforded a huge amount of respect for their sacrifice on our behalf. Similarly, Paralympians also receive a great deal of respect for their achievements. Then, again it's only my view, people who have become disabled through industrial injury or a road traffic accident – an occurrence that wasn't their fault but has left them with a life-changing injury – sees a blurring of the emotion between sympathy for what has happened and respect for how they are dealing with it. The final group are those who have inherited disability, those people who have no explanation as to why they have an impairment. In many cases, the level of disability is often much higher than those whose impairment has been acquired. Many in this group are unable to look after themselves and require the support of carers and, ultimately, the state in order to have a quality of life. These people have had to fight for everything in life – the right level of education, appropriate housing and the right level of benefits to support them. Yet they are amongst the group of disabled people in our society who receive the majority of the hate, the discrimination and prejudice. I'm not saying at all that people with disabilities in the other groups do not experience hate and discrimination, it is more my point that they receive much more respect from the general population than the last group.

I have been fortunate not to have experienced too much hate throughout my life. Two examples are that, once, whilst driving to London I was overtaken by a group of lads in a car. They had seen the Powerchair in the back of my car and as they passed, they were making distorted faces, licking the windows of their car and making gestures and laughing at how funny they were being. The second example took place at Lord's. I'd parked my car outside of the ECB offices and was removing the Powerchair from the back of my car. There was a group of people on a tour of Lord's who were making their way towards the Lord's shop when I heard one young lad say, "Look out, here come the spackers." I looked at him straightaway and stared. He looked away giggling because it was clear that I'd heard him.

I was astounded and disappointed in both cases. It goes to prove that this sort of abuse still exists. There may well have been other examples of where I have been discriminated against because of disability but I have not recognised it as such.

I have tried to take the approach that if an individual is wearing a pair of glasses, then it is because they have a weakness of some description in their eyes. If a person is using a wheelchair, then there is a weakness or loss of function that affects their legs. Either way, both impairments need an aid to restore functionality. But one is classed as disabled and the other is not.

For the last 15 years of their life together, Mum and Dad would just not listen to Paul and me. Their stubbornness and intransigence was a car crash waiting to happen. Dad's strength and mobility was deteriorating, and he had become completely reliant on Mum. Mum had essentially become a full-time carer, but would not accept any of the help that was on offer to her for fear of upsetting Dad, who was still adamant that he was not disabled and didn't need help.

The key to any intervention is consent. Dad would not agree that he needed the help that Mum was giving him on a daily basis, therefore Mum could not access the support that she desperately needed from the Carers Service or Social Services. Mum would not ask for help for fear of upsetting Dad. Paul and I saw this perfect storm brewing over many years and felt absolutely helpless. Without the consent of my parents, local Social Services were pretty much powerless to help.

Paul and I both struggled mentally with the situation. We could see what was happening but could do nothing about it. We were watching our parents descend into an entirely avoidable black hole. Every time we raised a concern with them, the conversation deteriorated into a row. There was no enjoyment in going to visit Mum and Dad. Dad wouldn't say anything, the TV volume was on its maximum because his hearing had gone (he refused to wear hearing aids), Mum constantly complained about how pig-headed Dad had become and how her life was awful. You'd offer some solutions but there was always a reason why this or that wouldn't work for them.

Mum had taken to enjoying perhaps more wine than is healthy and dad was falling more often than ever before. If only he would use a wheelchair or his scooter around the house. Mum could not lift Dad when he fell. They'd been given lifting equipment but either didn't know how to use it properly or it was unsuitable for Dad with his lack of core stability. Mum would ask anyone who was around to help pick Dad up, neighbours, postmen, UPS Delivery Drivers, anyone who happened to be in the neighbourhood. I found this appalling on two levels: firstly, the lack of dignity for Dad and secondly, the fact that if any of these helpers injured themselves lifting Dad, they would be bringing stress into their lives all because my dad was too proud to use a wheelchair. This didn't register with Dad at all. It got to the point where Paul and I were never told when Dad had fallen. Quite often, the only way we would find out would be if we spoke to their neighbours, who I have to say have been just the most supportive, magnificent people we could have asked for to be living next to our parents. To this day, I have no idea how often my dad was picked up off the floor by someone outside of our family – we were never told the half of it.

In 2017, Joanna and I were preparing for Conor to go on a school trip to do some sports-coaching in South Africa. I'd been able to acquire some cricket equipment and we set off from home to drop the kit off with Conor's PE Teacher. Returning to the house, I saw my Uncle Ken walking down the road towards our house. As I slowed the car down to greet my uncle, I said to Conor, "There's no good news coming out of this."

Kenny had gone to Mum and Dad's to visit as he often did. Mum wasn't there and when he asked where she was, Dad said she had gone to hospital. It turned out that she'd gotten up in the night to go to the toilet and tripped on the Kermode that they kept in the bedroom for Dad to use. She dislocated her shoulder but rather than call an ambulance then, she went back to bed. When she was unsurprisingly still in agony in the morning, she called an ambulance. Kenny was on his way to tell me because Dad had refused to call either me or Paul – unbelievable.

To make matters worse for us, we were due to drive to Keele University as Joanna was due to graduate from her master's degree that afternoon. Paul, of course, still knew nothing about any of this and the only reason that I knew was because my uncle insisted that I needed to.

They operated on Mum that day and pinned her shoulder back together. She was home within a couple of days. Kenny stayed with Dad whilst Mum was in hospital. Having Mum home was a relief in one way but just brought a whole load more stress for us all. We now had a dad who needed full-time care, and a Mum who was unable to care for him because she needed to rehabilitate herself and only had one effective arm. And, of course, neither of them wanted any help from anyone. No doubt Mum would enjoy a glass of wine now that she was back home and completely deny that it was the effect of a tipple that led to the fall in the first place.

Paul, Joanna and myself were exasperated at this point. There was a feeling amongst us that we'd dodged a bullet because things could have been much worse, but this was a clear warning shot to Mum and Dad that they could not carry on burying their heads in the sand regarding their situation.

Things came to a head in 2018. Dad had been diagnosed as Type 2 Diabetic and Coeliac some years previously. True to form he ignored every piece of advice given to him by a Dr regarding diet and he and Mum just carried on as normal. His health deteriorated greatly after Christmas in 2017. He lost any strength he had left. He was jaundice, indicating a problem with his liver. Every time he tried to get out of bed, he fell. The paramedics were out to him every day just to get him off the floor, after he had fallen, and back into bed. I'm not even going to talk about the toileting situation which was just horrendous for my Mum.

It was clear to all of us that Dad was very close to the end; he looked dreadful. Clear to all except Mum and Dad of course. I sat with Dad and asked if he would like to go to hospital to receive the care that my Mum was now unable to give him. When he replied yes, I thought, *jeez, he must feel rough*. Dad would never knowingly put himself in front of the medical profession. We got the Dr out to see him and he referred him to hospital straight away.

Almost immediately, he was diagnosed with decompensated liver disease. The prognosis was not good. Best estimate at that stage was that Dad had no longer than three months, at best, to live. Had he stayed at home, I'm not sure he'd have seen the week out.

Getting Dad into hospital was a big relief for us. But every silver lining has a cloud. We now had Mum at home on her own. Her reason for being, over the last 10 years at least, was caring for my dad. Dad was no longer there so what was she going to do? We all hoped that she would recover some of her love of life that had clearly been lost over the years. She had, over recent years, been to Tai Chi classes and maybe she'd pick that back up again. She loved reading and surely, she would enjoy having complete control over the TV remote for once.

Jo and I, Paul and Uncle Kenny and Aunty Pat took it in turns to ferry her to and from the hospital to see Dad. Sadly, for me at least, these trips were an emotional nightmare. There was just no talking to Mum. It had become clear to our close family that Mum was starting to suffer with memory loss. The most obvious evidence of this was one day when Paul had taken her shopping and she complained when she got to the till that someone had taken all her shopping out of the basket because there were so few items in it.

Taking her to see Dad was mental. He couldn't hear what she was saying and she couldn't remember either what he'd said to her or what she'd said to him. It was so stressful. We'd all be exhausted after a visit. But of course there was no talking to her. I lost track of the times she flew at me when I raised the question of her drinking or her memory.

I had been dealing with the solicitors with regards to Power of Attorney for Dad once it was decided that he would not be returning home. Mum phoned me up whilst I was working down in London to tell me that she knew what I was trying to do and she would never allow me to steal money from my dad; she was ashamed of me. I was devastated and really upset. I didn't sleep that night.

What if she had told others that was what she thought I was doing? Next day, I called her and asked her if she recalled the conversation and the allegations she had made. She didn't recall a thing. She simply said sorry and that was the matter closed.

Another time, I got a call from Aunty Pat who had taken Mum to see Dad. Pat told me that there had been a conversation between them and I hadn't fared too well out of it. She suggested that I went to see Dad. I visited Dad and asked if he was OK. He replied, "No, I'm not. What right have you got to employ lawyers from London to take money away from your Mum?"

This was madness on another level. I asked him if he honestly believed that and he said that's what Mum had told him.

Naturally, I went to see Mum. She denied all knowledge of the conversation. I told her that I no longer wanted anything to do with the POA or their bank accounts. It was so distressing. In her confusion, Mum had accused me of trying to steal from Dad and trying to get lawyers to stop her accessing his money. I was devastated; why would my own mum think that I'd do that?

Dad has been in a nursing home for two years now. He is unable to get out of bed, although he is still of sound mind as his almost daily grumbles about life testify. For someone who's been given three months maximum to live, he's holding out really well. Like I mentioned earlier, he's a stubborn bugger.

Whilst things came to head between 2017 and 2019, the whole situation has been upsetting and distressing for much longer. Paul and I never ended up living our adult lives having the relationship with our parents that many others enjoy. That said, we are not the only people experiencing similar things. How you perceive things is your reality and you can only control the controllables. I found taking that approach to a situation so close and personal, really difficult. We do not want to see people that we care about suffer or making, in our opinion, poor decisions. So we try and try to help, advise and convince our loved ones to take a different route, or think about things in a different way. In my case, I was dealing with two people who had adopted almost a siege mentality. It felt at times like they were saying it was just them vs the system and the outside world. Every time a solution was suggested, they would find a reason why that wouldn't work for them. It was exhausting. In hindsight, both my brother and I spent far too long trying to help two people who were never going to allow themselves to be helped. In the process we caused ourselves untold stress and worry.

Through the process, we encountered the ethical maze of consent and capacity. Dad retained the capacity to make his own decisions. He still has that capacity. Mum, on the other hand, was really struggling to make logical decisions and her refusal to attend a Memory Clinic, as recommended by her GP, made getting any diagnosis impossible. Without a diagnosis, nobody could take action to improve her mental state. The law around capacity allows for those deemed of sound mind to be able to make their own decisions about their financial affairs and their medical treatment. As we discovered, this also allows them the right to make what we may consider to be poor decisions.

Dad struggled on his admittance to hospital to adapt to the environment or the routine of the ward that he was on. They immediately put him on a Coeliac diet. He decided to go on a hunger strike because the "food was shit". Our amazing NHS had brought him back from the brink but he was acting like a complete buffoon. We would go and visit and find that he'd abused nurses, refused food, and on one occasion, refused to be treated by a nurse of an ethnic background. I was disgusted with him. His physical appearance at this time made him almost unrecognisable as my dad, but worse for me was his behaviour.

I found myself losing respect for him because of his attitude towards himself and others. He had no grasp of the impact of his decisions on my Mum. In my view, he became extremely selfish. By regularly falling over at home, he was putting others at risk when they helped to pick him up. It is not the job of a postman to be picking up a dead-weight of a person that he comes across. Falling became a regular event when once it was an occasional occurrence, but Dad never adapted his approach to his changing situation.

Through my work, I regularly saw people with far higher levels of disability having a far better quality of life. Dad, for some reason, could not cope with being labelled disabled. The irony of that is that his attitude made him more disabled than anyone else I know.

There was a period of time when Dad just couldn't be trusted to stay safe if Mum went out to the shops, for example. She'd come home and find him in the garage, using a blowtorch to weld something together. Heaven knows what would have happened if he'd have fallen whilst using that. Dad just didn't see the issue.

I was resentful over the fact that I didn't have the relationship with my parents that I wanted. It really upset me to see what they had turned into.

Mum spent the last years of her life as a nervous wreck because of Dad. Paul and I only got glimpses of what it must have been like because they never told us anything, and visiting had become such an ordeal that we never stayed long. If Mum phoned after 6 pm at night, I never answered the phone. Invariably, she would be under the influence and completely irrational. I lost count of the amount of times that she'd call and I'd end up emotionally drained at the end of it. I had to stop answering the phone for my own sanity.

My parents were really decent, fun-loving people but I believe that the disability, or rather their approach to dealing with it, robbed me of my relationship with them. Sometimes we are just not self-aware enough to understand the impact of our behaviours on others. I tried to change my approach towards them. I tried to accept that they would never change and that I should stop trying to help them, because I got really upset every time I tried to help and it wasn't accepted or appreciated. It's human nature to try and help those you love and it's heartbreaking to watch people you care about head towards a completely avoidable car crash. My parents had absolutely no idea that their behaviour was crushing their sons.

Mum had developed a "why us" attitude. She became really bitter about what had happened to Dad and her two boys because of this disease. She just couldn't get her head around it. She needed answers, a reason and a point of blame. She often said to me that I could blame my dad for me having it and couldn't understand that I wasn't looking for or needing something to blame.

I was down in London on 14th January 2019, ready for a Cap Presentation Ceremony to some of ECB's International Disabled Players the next day. That evening, I was preparing to have dinner at The Ivy in St John's Wood with Richard, Edgar, Bradders and Ackers. I decided to call home before I went out. Jo told me that she was in A&E with my Mum who had fallen and broken her hip. They would operate on her the next day.

Mum had been to visit Dad that afternoon and had returned home. She had no idea that she'd seen him for the last time. I have no doubt that she would have enjoyed a glass or two of wine that afternoon and she decided to put the recycling out for collection the next morning. It was a wintry day and gust of wind made her lose her balance whilst handling the garden waste bin. She fell and broke her hip. Thankfully, her neighbours saw her lying on the ground and contacted Joanna.

The first thing that the Drs noticed was that there was alcohol in Mum's system, and given that she had a stay in hospital ahead of her with no access to alcohol, they needed to give her drugs to reduce her dependency on it and to be able to treat her effectively. They operated on her hip on 15th January. The operation was successful, and she returned to the ward. Sometime later that day, she suffered a heart attack. Her body was so weak that it had struggled to cope with the stress of the fall and the operation. Mum was stabilised but the Drs said her heart was only operating at 20% of its capacity.

Over the next two weeks, Mum was drifting in and out of consciousness, and even when she was awake she was largely incoherent. All the family came to visit her and she was able to recognise everybody which was great, but it was clear that she was in a bad way.

The only person unable to see her was Dad. Paul and I now had the unenviable task of having to try and visit both parents, in two separate medical institutions that were 15 miles apart. The heartbreaking element of this was that they couldn't even talk to each other on the phone. Dad's hearing had gone, and Mum was incoherent at best.

Dad was hopeful, as we all were I guess, that after the operation Mum would be OK and on the road to recovery. Sitting and telling him that Mum was very poorly and slowly slipping away from us was the hardest thing I have ever had to do. They'd celebrated their 50th Wedding Anniversary only a few months before and now he had to face up to the fact that he would not be seeing or even hearing from her again. I'd never seen him shed a tear in my life, he was very much of the generation where men didn't cry. Watching him fill up with tears was incredibly difficult to watch. I was emotionally drained (again) after leaving him that day.

One of their last conversations, on the Sunday afternoon before Mum fell, concerned a local butcher who had suddenly passed away. Mum had explained about his passing but wasn't able to tell Dad the name of the butcher (memory issues). Dad was concerned that it might have been the butcher that they had frequented for the previous 15 years. It turned out it wasn't.

A couple of days later, Dad passed me a letter that he had written to Mum and asked me to pass it to her on my next visit to the hospital. Jo and I looked across the room at each other, thinking how romantic but also how sad this was. Dad used to write Mum poetry when they first got together, and I thought it was lovely that in these really dark moments he'd taken the time to write some words of love and comfort to her. It felt like I was seeing a side of my parents' relationship that I'd not seen before. I was impressed with Dad. Not only had I seen some actual emotion from him, I'd also seen a romantic side that had never previously surfaced. To give this some context, this is a bloke who once bought Mum a new iron for Christmas – this is what we were dealing with here.

I had no idea about the content of what Dad had written. He'd sealed his letter in an envelope and written 'Pam' in his barely legible faint handwriting on the front. Jo and I were both intrigued to know what he'd written and were excited when we got to the hospital ward that evening to see Mum.

She had been moved to the Cardiac ward to continue her treatment and it seemed, by her animation upon our arrival, that her condition had improved slightly. "Thank God you're here, get me out of this place I want to go home," she shouted. "It's falling apart, it's a hellhole and nobody knows what they are doing." Mum was never shy of exaggeration, but this seemed a little excessive, even by her standards. We calmed her down and eventually passed her the letter from Dad.

Jo and I waited, either side of her bed with bated breath. What magical words of comfort, support and compassion had Dad sent to his poorly wife?

Mum read the note and put it in the drawer at the side of the bed. She never told us what was written and never showed any emotion at all.

That's all a bit of an anticlimax, I thought. I was desperate to look at what had been written but left the note where it was out of respect to them both. It was quite clearly private.

On the evening of 28th January, Jo and I sat with Mum for the last time. She was fast asleep and I'm not sure that she knew we were there at all. My lasting memory of that evening was that she was snoring really loudly. She was making a noise that wouldn't have been out of place at an African watering hole after the drought had ended. There was nothing of her, she looked so frail, but the noise was unbelievable. *Nothing wrong with her lungs,* I thought. I held her hand, gave it a kiss and said goodbye.

The telephone rang at 5:20 am the next morning. The nurse said that Mum's breathing pattern had changed and that we should come in. Jo and I arrived at the hospital at just gone 6 am. Mum had passed peacefully in her sleep about 20 minutes earlier.

I didn't feel sad, certainly didn't cry, but felt strangely relieved that she was now at peace and was going to get the rest that had been denied her in her retirement. I phoned Paul to tell him and asked if he would go to the nursing home and tell Dad, as I had some formalities to complete at the hospital. "I'm not sure I can do that," he replied.

Before we left the hospital to go and see Dad, there was one thing I had to do. I really wanted to see that letter that Dad had written. I opened the drawer next to Mum's bed to remove her effects and there was the letter. It read

Dear Pam,

Just to let you know that Stevie Vaughan wasn't the butcher that died. Hope you're feeling better soon.

Love, Brian

My Dad. Absolutely priceless.

Mental Health

After returning home from tours, I'd noticed that my mood always became very low for a few days, maybe even a couple of weeks. Here are some journal notes that I made after returning home from Australia in 2015.

Struggling

Been home for two days. I don't feel happy. This is a recurring cycle every time that I come home from a tour. The first evening is great, we are all glad that I am home. The kids are made up because I bring them presents back. For me, after that it goes downhill. I don't know whether it is post-tour blues, the downer you hit after a successful tour or whether it is the effects of jet lag. I just don't know but I am very irritable, and Conor is bearing the brunt of it.

Joanna is working so in addition to being away from home for the best part of three weeks, I have had no time with her since I got back because she is working. The children are on Easter holidays and Conor spent eight hours yesterday on his play station. I was not happy. We went to my mum's so that I could show Mum and Dad my pictures. Not a great experience. The only comment Dad made about the photos was that one or two of the lads were overweight and then he asked what the score was in the series. So, with more social media coverage than we have ever had, my own parents hadn't been able to find out what the scores were or follow how we'd got on. I got the impression from Dad that he was disappointed that I hadn't emailed him every day with updates. I didn't get into the reasons why I had no time to be emailing updates, besides which, what is the point of there being a media officer on tour and providing all these updates if I still need to send personal emails. Very frustrating.

I've come back home after what has been a real emotional rollercoaster of a tour – the challenge of managing the staff/tour, the professional success of winning 5-1 in Australia, the anxiety of four days on my own and wondering how I'd cope and the excitement of coming home. Not one person has asked me how

I am. I've had no time with Jo and all I feel that I am doing is alienating my son. I feel hopeless and useless as a parent. Jo has just had the best part of three weeks on her own, looking after the two kids and working full-time and now I come home, and my state must make things harder for her. It is at times like this in the past when I feel as if I am better off not being around.

I feel like I'm a bit of a mess at the moment and completely anti-social. I don't want to make small talk with anyone. I don't think I know anyone outside of the guys that I was away with, who can have any understanding of how I feel. If anyone asks me how my holiday was, I feel likely to explode.

I'm tired. I have so much work to do that will all be waiting for me when I get back. What is the point of taking leave? I feel that Conor is just wasting his life, sitting in front of the PlayStation. It's just a ridiculous amount of time that he spends on there. I am struggling to cope with the guilt of letting him know my dissatisfaction with his behaviour – I think he just thinks that I don't like him when all I am trying to do his improve him. Why can't I just let him be. Why can't I be happy with who he is. I read his school report today and everybody said that he is just a lovely lad, popular in class and who tries really hard. I was so proud of him. So why can't I just let him be?

My head is fog.

Whilst in Australia, I spent a lot of time on my scooter. Since I have been home, I haven't walked great distances and have not used my scooter or my sticks at all. My back is killing me, and I just want to lie down all the time. I am frightened about how poor my legs have become. I feel like a fall is possible every step I take and like I have no strength at all.

Talk about highs and lows and ups and downs.

As I mentioned earlier, I was 12 in 1982. Britain had sent its Navy, Army and Air Force to the Falkland Islands in the South Atlantic to reclaim the islands from Argentinian occupation. I can remember vividly, watching the news bulletins bring news back into our homes as to how the fighting was progressing. I remember watching in disbelief when HMS Sheffield was hit and then in awe as the Royal Marines marched across the Islands prior to the final battle to recover Port Stanley.

One of my most vivid memories was watching the evening news at home on 8th June 1982. Simon Weston, as you may know, is one of this country's heroes. He was a Welsh Guardsman who was onboard Sir Galahad waiting to land on the Falkland Islands in 1982 as part of the UK Task Force sent by the Government.

As the Welsh Guards were preparing to land, Sir Galahad came under attack and three bombs hit and a huge fire engulfed the ship. 48 people died and many others were very badly injured. Fortunately, Simon survived despite having 46% burns and became one of the UK's most prominent war veterans. I found him inspirational, I'd read most of his books and I was very aware of his story and how he obtained his injuries.

So, when I had the opportunity to attend a presentation that he was giving at the ECB's elite coaches conference, I was undecided on whether I should go. What was I going to learn that I didn't already know about this amazing bloke?

I ended up going along. Simon is a great speaker, really engaging. It's hard not to be affected by his story when you read it or hear him talking about his experiences. Imagine being with your mates, preparing to go into the unknown, the banter, the fear, the excitement… and then boom, you're in a hell, consumed by fire and smoke. The trauma is almost unimaginable, but the Welsh Guards lived it on 8th June 1982. I read about this so many times and sat in the conference unmoved by Simon retelling the story of what happened. I didn't know it, but my awakening was about to come.

Simon moved on to talk about his repatriation back to the UK and the start of his rehabilitation and his discharge from the Army on medical grounds. As he recalled his experiences of how the military dealt with his discharge, I could feel a whole load of emotion welling up inside of me. He articulated everything that I experienced when I was released from the Navy. I felt horrible and didn't understand what was going on, tears started coming down my face and I had to get out of the room where Simon was talking. I got outside and found a table. I was trembling and crying uncontrollably. What the hell was going on? I didn't understand what had happened to me. It was really strange but in that moment, I was back at RNH Haslar being told that I had no future in the Navy – the shame, the rejection, the lack of respect, the anger, the loss of identity and the feeling of worthlessness had come back and slapped me in the face. 20 odd years of suppressing all that anger and emotion in order to get on with my life was now confronting me in a corridor at St George's Park.

The next thing I remember was that I was being comforted by Rosie Mayes, a lovely lady and brilliant coach whom I had known for a few years. She clicked quite quickly as to what was going on and got me away to somewhere a bit more private. I can't remember much else about that evening; my head had turned to mush, and I wasn't even drinking. I woke up the next morning feeling like I'd been hit with a sledgehammer.

ECB's Head of Elite Coaching at the time was the brilliant Gordon Lord. He came and found me and offered me every support that our organisation could provide. He was brilliant. I still had no idea what had happened but every time I recalled Simon talking about losing his career and his identity, it set me off. It was so raw. It didn't seem to make any sense. My experience of war was very different to Simon's. I could not relate to, or begin to understand, the trauma that he went through, both on the Sir Galahad and throughout his rehabilitation. Yet there was something in the way that the Armed forces treated him that resonated with me on a level that awakened my subconscious, and all these demons that had bedded down there for years. The demons decided they wanted a party inside my mind and whilst they were making hay, I felt exhausted.

Lordy got me in touch with an organisation called Changing Minds and a Psychologist called Andy. Andy was very good. Over the course of the next 12 months, we unpacked a whole load of suppressed anger, grief, and upset relating to both my discharge from the Navy, my diagnosis and prognosis and the strained and deteriorating relationship with my parents. I felt as if I'd been laid bare, stripped naked and was extremely vulnerable. It felt like previously I was walking down a big, wide pavement and no matter what hit me, I never stumbled into the road. But now I was walking, balancing along the kerb and the slightest knock would see me fall into the oncoming traffic. I would cry at almost anything and I felt like a broken man. I felt worthless and of no use to anyone. I would have really self-defeating thoughts and then begin to ruminate and end up in a downward spiral to the point where I thought that Jo and the kids would be much better off without me bringing them down. The only place that I seemed to get any happiness was at work. I felt like I was worth something and that I was making a difference. I threw myself into work, spending more and more time away from home, and down in London. I was effectively running away from having to deal with Mum and Dad and the car crash that was waiting to happen and all of the upset they were causing me and my brother. This was never going to be the answer though because the more I was away, the less I was being a husband and a dad. I felt guilty yet didn't change and just felt worse about myself. Writing about it now, it all seems a bit dramatic but that is how I was.

I heard a saying that a broken crayon still works. That is how I felt. I was definitely broken but still ploughing on.

It has taken a while for me to start to value myself again. I'd given myself a really hard time for a long time. I'd gotten into a mindset, not long after I was discharged from the Navy, that I would never lose a job again because of my disability. The only thing that I had control of was how hard I worked, and I decided that I would work harder than anyone else so that no employer would ever want to release me. I guess it's kind of like the glass ceiling that female employees talk about – you have to work twice as hard to get noticed or promoted. In my mind, I was working hard just to stand still and not to experience the rejection again. The problem was that I hadn't realised what was happening to me.

I can recall being in a bad way immediately after I came out of the Navy. I had no idea what to do with my life and the lifestyle change was a real shock to the system. I don't recall spending any time thinking how the experience had affected me. Andy at Changing Minds unlocked a whole load of feelings and emotions that I must have slammed into a box in the back of my mind within a few weeks of leaving the Navy. I think I moved quite quickly from being down on my luck and upset about my treatment to getting into a headspace that allowed me to move forward and start again. Within a couple months of being a civvy, I'd met my future wife and was looking forward not backwards.

On one level, this was brilliant and just what I needed but the flip side was that my mind had not processed or dealt with the bitterness and the anger that I felt towards the Navy. Maybe I was too young and immature to be able to deal with the disappointment of my diagnosis and subsequent discharge from the Navy. I felt like a failure and that I had been rejected. I believe now that my subconscious buried these feelings until I was better able to deal with them but that it also gave me a fear of rejection which has shaped my motivations and work ethic since. I had a drive to be the best, to win and to succeed, and everything was great when this occurred. However, not everyone wins all the time and those that seek perfection are never going to be happy because they always want more. And so, the fear of rejection set me up to fail in many ways because I was never able to be satisfied with what I had achieved – I always wanted more.

It's taken me 26 years to figure out how I work and what makes me click. I've learned that there are more ways to win in life than winning alone. I'm at peace now with the fact that the Navy had to let me go, they had no choice. Although I still believe the whole thing could have been handled better.

I would never have believed that one of the heroes I watched on the TV as a 12-year-old would end up having such a profound impact on my life many years later. I hit rock bottom after listening to him speak, but sometimes you have to take a hit to come back stronger.

I've heard people say that it's not easy going to get help. In my case it wasn't a big deal at all. I'd been experiencing periodic bouts of feeling really low for quite a while. It mainly came about when I'd be fed up with myself for not handling Conor in a better way. I hated the way that I'd lose patience and my temper with him when he didn't do things that I'd asked him to do, or he didn't do things quickly enough or well enough. I always felt as if he was letting himself down and I couldn't bear to see it happening. The reality was that he was just a kid, doing the things that adolescent teenage boys do.

I hated myself for the way that I was with him. It felt like my will for him to make the best of himself versus his teenage angst and lethargy. I'd try and try to be better but I failed, and I struggled to deal with not being able to control my responses to his triggers. We'd fall out, we'd both get upset – I was the adult and should have been able to manage situations better and I hated myself because I couldn't.

The feeling of inadequacy was then exacerbated by my physical limitations. I couldn't put the bins out; I couldn't mow the lawn. My disability was getting worse and I was really starting to notice it. For years I'd ploughed on regardless, but now I have to think about everything that I do, everywhere I go. Can I get a parking spot? Is there an accessible entrance? Where are the toilets, are they upstairs? For the first time in my life, it was really getting me down. Everything about this disability now impacts my wife and children, when I always vowed that it wouldn't. I was kidding myself. When it's icy, I don't even leave the house now for fear of slipping and falling. If I damage my wrist, my arm or my hands, I'd be completely screwed because I need to use them to stand up. I can't get out of a chair without using my arms. If I fall, I am unable to get up off the floor by myself.

In the month after returning from South Africa and the Blind Cricket World Cup in December 2014, I fell badly, twice. One time I was just returning from my shed and I slipped on some ice on one of the paving slabs in the garden. I was on the floor for about 15 minutes whilst Conor and Jo sorted out the portable lifting device that I have been given. It was freezing. The second fall was more serious. I fell in our bedroom and banged the back of my head on our wardrobe and badly hurt my knee and my foot, which twisted as I fell. I went into shock and was lying shivering and shaking in agony on the floor. Ciara cried her eyes out. Conor was on his PlayStation. Jo had nipped to the shops. I lay there, unable to move or to even straighten my leg. My head was pounding and I remember wondering how hard you had to bang your head before knocking yourself out. Jo came home and she and Conor set up the inflatable lifting device and put me to bed. I felt pathetic and useless.

It just accumulated, I felt like a crap father, a crap husband and unable to change things, whilst knowing that it was only me that could change things. Then I look at myself and think, come on, get a grip of yourself and stop feeling sorry for yourself, man up. It feels like there are two sides to my personality – the confident, bolshy, happy and fun-loving side and the vulnerable, never happy, self-critical perfectionist side.

Add all this to the Simon Weston episode that unearthed all of the anger and bitterness that I had clearly not dealt with after my discharge from the Navy, and it started to become clear to me that I wasn't quite right.

I was never happy. Nothing was ever good enough; when I achieved something I always wanted more. Why couldn't I be happy with what I had? Why couldn't I enjoy the here and now without wanting more and better? It seems like the same drivers that have led me to achieve and be successful were now causing me to be unhappy. I wanted to be the perfect dad and husband and manager and in reality who is that perfect? I was in pursuit of an impossible dream that I will never achieve. I've spent life since my diagnosis and subsequent discharge from the Navy wanting to prove that I was not the write-off that the Navy made me feel.

Not sure who I was trying to prove things to – the Navy certainly didn't give a toss. Maybe it was Dad who used to circle jobs in the paper that he thought I should go for just after I left the Navy. My head was well and truly up my arse at that point. I had just lost my job, my identity, my purpose and suffered the subsequent loss of confidence and self-esteem. It was a huge feeling of rejection. I had been diagnosed with a disability that was only going to get worse and Dad was giving me shit about not getting a job as a labourer to get some money. It wasn't what I needed. I needed time and space to sort my head out. It felt to me as if Dad saw me as a bit of a waster at that point in my life. I was claiming the benefits that I was entitled to, that I had paid into, but this was an alien concept to Dad. He was of the generation that never wanted to claim dole. To be honest, I didn't either, but I wasn't going to be rushing into some dead-end job. I wanted to keep my options open. I was as proud as he was, it just showed itself in a different way.

I wanted to do things my way and whether his suggestions were right or not, I think I had got myself into a headspace that I would do the opposite for the spite of it. I was fed up of being told what to do, and then, that I would amount to nothing much.

So, maybe all this time I've been trying to prove him wrong. I don't know. I do know that I have achieved and been successful everywhere that I have worked including the Navy. I have never settled for what I have started with and always worked and achieved more. So, maybe this drive for self-improvement and betterment has always been there and proving something or somebody wrong hasn't been the motivator. I can't answer the question but what I did know was that if I didn't find some level of happiness with what I have got, then I would die unhappy and unsatisfied.

I have been really fortunate with the help that I received when I was at my lowest. I talked earlier about the help that I received from Andy at Changing Minds following my meltdown after listening to Simon Weston. When things started getting really stressful and coming to a head with my parents' health, ECB supported me once again and I have been working with another practitioner from Changing Minds named Shreeta who has also been of great support.

There has been a huge shift in the perception of mental health over the last few years. As a society we have a much greater awareness of PTSD and we are beginning to accept that mental health problems can affect any of us at any time. Hopefully, I'm over the worst of the struggles that I have had, although I can be prone to low mood and the occasional feelings of worthlessness, but not at the level or seriousness that I experienced before. I still talk to Shreeta now and again as I feel I need to and I also talk to a local lady, Kate Morris-Bates, who runs a company called Inside-Wellness in Mold. Kate has been brilliant and has really challenged my thinking and understanding of myself.

I've learned things about myself from each of these amazing people. Andy opened up a box of emotion, frustration and anger that I thought I'd sealed the lid on relating to my discharge from the Navy. He also made me realise that trying to be a perfectionist was a pretty impossible dream. He explained that my pursuit of excellence was pretty typical of people who had worked in the military or in elite sport. I had done both and he suggested that for my own health my ambitions needed to be managed, or at the very least, approached differently. I have since recognised through my work with Kate that the root cause of this potentially damaging strive for perfection is a fear of failure or rejection. As an adolescent, I didn't receive much positive reinforcement from Dad. As I grew older and took a different path to the one I think he wanted for me, he would call me a jammy bugger when I'd achieved something, rather than saying: "Well done, you've earned that success." This was followed by the biggest and most damaging rejection that I suffered – discharge from the Navy. Since then, it seems that I have been driven by not wanting to feel that pain of rejection again.

Shreeta made me recognise that I was running on empty. My emotional bucket was full. Between 2018 and 2020, Dad's condition worsened. Mum could no longer look after him. Neither of them would admit it. Mum was drinking more and more. Dad got diagnosed with liver disease and was admitted to a nursing home. Mum's condition worsened and dementia became obvious. Mum accused me of using the Power of Attorney to empty Dad's bank account and then told Dad that I had appointed lawyers in London to prevent her accessing Dad's money – false and hugely upsetting accusations which she then couldn't remember making. Mum then fell and broke her hip. Mum was in hospital and Dad in a nursing home, 15 miles apart. Dad couldn't hear what Mum said and Mum couldn't remember what Dad said – phone calls were useless. Mum passed away in hospital without speaking with Dad in the last two weeks of her life. There was the funeral to arrange, the estate to settle and house to sell. Dad was really upset and wanted me to send him to Dignitas in Switzerland to die. He told me he wanted to commit suicide and went on hunger strike in his nursing home.

Whilst all this was going on, Joanna and I were trying to manage our own family. Conor finished school and was commuting up to Manchester every day to college. Ciara was in high school. I was travelling back and forward to London every week and also trying to visit Dad as often as I could. Jo's dad was in and out of hospital with heart trouble. It was never-ending. The summer after Mum passed away, Conor moved away to University in Worcester. It's a special time for any parent to see their children moving on and making their own way in life, but with everything else going on, it felt like just another event we had to deal with.

Not wanting to look a failure for not being able to cope with all of this, I just ploughed on. With hindsight, I can see that I spent more time in London than perhaps I needed to. I threw myself into work because it was a huge distraction from everything else that was going on. Work was something I felt successful with and I felt as if I was making a difference when there were so many other areas of my life where I felt worthless and pathetic.

So I guess Shreeta didn't need all of her Psychology experience to recognise that my bucket was full and clearly overflowing. The important thing is to recognise when you are struggling and to get help. There's no prizes for suffering and struggling. We all have a mental health state – it's a scale; at one end we are buzzing and at the other we are in a very dark place – we all take our place at some place between those two points. Different things affect different people in different ways. In my experience, the psychologists don't take the issues away, they are not magicians, they make you appreciate things and look at things from a different perspective. They allow you to come up for air and find some space to explore and explain how you feel and why. I can honestly say talking has worked for me and objective, unbiased and different perspectives have helped me find answers to issues that I sometimes didn't know I had, which in turn have helped me deal with the more obvious challenges in a much better way.

All I know is that I got help and support from people who listened. They weren't conversations that I wanted to have with Joanna. She sees everyday how I manage, how I struggle and shares my frustration. The impact of my fluctuating mental health was something that I didn't want to burden her with. Although, having said that, she was experiencing the impact of it anyway; the low moods and the grumpiness. Her strength has been remarkable through everything, she gives everything to me and our children and asks for nothing. I'm a lucky fella.

The more you open up about mental health, I have found that it helps others to do the same. I'm not saying that you disclose your life story to a guy next to you on the tube, but when the environment is right and you are with people you trust, I guarantee you'll help yourself by sharing and potentially help them feel safe enough to share their experiences too. None of us are alone with these things. Reach out if you need to.

I've experienced a lot of ups and downs throughout my life. You may be familiar with the poem "If" by Rudyard Kipling. For me it is one of the great writings. It is about self-control and managing your emotions and reactions to different experiences. When I was younger, I never understood how powerful emotional control is – getting it wrong impairs your actions, your responses and your ability to function effectively. As we get older, we develop a greater sense of perspective and become better able to rationalise and manage our emotional state.

As I look back, I can see that I was fortunate in some ways in terms of the experiences that I had. But was I fortunate, or did I allow myself exposure to such experiences by virtue of the choices that I made?

By the age of 18, I'd been around the world getting well-paid in the Navy. By 21, I'd seen active service in the first Gulf War. At 22, I was diagnosed with a life changing disability and by 24, I'd been released by the Navy and my life turned completely upside down.

All of those experiences, relatively early in my life, have provided me with a reference point when I experience disappointments or encounter difficulties now. I've not experienced anything as frightening as being under attack in the Gulf – so that upcoming budget deadline, that I am still in control of, is not as stressful as my boss or a colleague is making it sound.

My reference points are a bit extreme, not everyone will have been under attack at sea or have been diagnosed with a disability but we all have had experiences that enable us to contextualise.

I will volunteer for things that others back away from. What can possibly go wrong? If it does go wrong, at the very least I will have learnt something. There have been many examples in my life where I have just thrown my hat in the ring and I have benefited. Dad always used to call me a "Jammy Bastard". I resented that because whatever experiences or opportunities I had were as a result of choices that I made. Similarly, on the occasions where I have come to regret things that I have done, there is no blame involved – I've made the decisions and I take the responsibility.

It is really important to me, at a values level, that people take responsibility and ownership for things that affect them. It is not unusual, and perhaps unsurprising, that people with a disability or their families in times of hardship/frustration ask themselves the question "Why Me?" or "Why Us?" In my view, these questions are defeatist and unhelpful. You'll never find an answer that satisfies you. When she was at her lowest with caring for my father, my mum would often say, "Why me?" or "why has this disease affected my husband and my boys?" She never found the answer and went to her grave wondering.

I believe that we are all products of our experiences. If you were sick the first time you went on a waltzer, you might be reluctant to go on one again. Even though you know that the majority of people don't have that reaction to the ride. Your personal experience wasn't great so it could put you off doing it again.

If you apply that rule to all the experiences that we have in life, it is easy to see why adults are less adaptable to change than children are. Adults have reference points as a result of their experiences whereas children don't – essentially they are fearless.

The point that I'm getting to here is that the vast majority of adults have some beliefs as a result of their experience that will limit them in reaching their potential or growth. So it is not a physical obstacle to development or growth but a mental one based on fear. These are beliefs that we are in control of and can take ownership of because fear is nothing more than an unhelpful and limiting emotion.

Don't get me wrong, I'm no self–help guru but positivity and accountability has allowed me to take control of my life in a major way. As soon as you take ownership and responsibility for your actions, and stop either waiting for others or blaming others for what's wrong, your life becomes much easier to manage and much less confrontational.

During the time that I have worked in Disability Sport, and in cricket in particular, I have learnt so much about myself. It sounds strange to say but I know who I am and I am comfortable with that person. I didn't always feel that way. In my mind I was always trying to be the best that I could be, always had my foot to the floor trying to prove to someone (I had no idea who), that despite my disability I could be as good or better than anyone else. It was like I was fighting the past experience of being released by the Navy, desperate to prove that I was not a failure and that I had something to offer, even if the Navy didn't want it.

I became a perfectionist. Dictionary definition noun: perfectionist; plural noun: perfectionists, a person who refuses to accept any standard short of perfection.

"He was a perfectionist who worked slowly"

Perfectionism, in psychology, is a broad personality style characterized by a person's concern with striving for flawlessness and perfection, and is accompanied by critical self-evaluations and concerns regarding others' evaluations (Wikipedia).

I was very much an example of the psychological personality type described above. We (England Disability Cricket) and I had to be the best at what we did. Sometimes it drove me to distraction. If things weren't right, I would self-analyse and self-criticise until I understood why. The feeling of something not being perfect worked two ways. Firstly, it provided the drive and motivation for me to make things better. But secondly, and more dangerously from a mental health perspective, the pursuit of perfection is never-ending and unattainable. This is because once you have delivered something or achieved something that you recognise as being exceptional, the brain starts to ask how can we make it better. Or, in the case of an Olympic Gold Medal winning athlete, you've reached the pinnacle, what do you do next? – the best you'll ever get in the future is another Gold.

I did a lot of self-reflection. The question of "Is good enough, good enough?" used to blow my mind. In a perfectionist mind, the question is answered with a simple No! In the mind of my teenage son who has dyslexia, Good Enough in an exam means it's time to crack open the champagne. They say every day is a school day and Conor's journey and experiences certainly helped me to re-evaluate my thinking.

Like most parents, I find both of my children exceptional in different ways. It is clear now that Conor has had dyslexia ever since he started school. I feel strongly that the education system in Wales let him down badly. Focus went on the high-achievers who were expected to get the top grades. Jo and I were told when Conor was in Year eight that it was extremely unlikely that he would make it to university. Language and words came easy to me, I loved reading when I was a kid. When he was growing up I couldn't understand why Conor didn't want to improve his reading – by reading. I know now that the very thought of it must have terrified him. I can't imagine what school must have been like for him. Going back to what I was saying before about experiences – he will have had experiences that I could never understand because of his dyslexia and therefore, he is perfectly placed to advise, support and educate others in this area. He got himself to university, he's just starting his 2nd year and we have seen him grow both physically and in confidence. He would never say it but he is determined and resilient – a chip off the old block I would like to say. The point I would like to make here is that although his dyslexia could be seen as a weakness, it has also given him a strength in that he can empathise with others like him who maybe lack confidence like he did, and he can certainly explain to others, such as myself, who cannot imagine what he has experienced because of a difficulty processing words and letters.

The temptation has always been to think "why me?" but I have just never thought like that. I've always thought that there is always someone worse off than me and that I shouldn't grumble, because at the end of the day, I've have had a decent life.

Because the condition has worsened gradually over time, my mind has been able adapt to the physical changes and my limitations in unison. Someone who acquires disability through industrial accident, or through a car accident for example, does not have this luxury. I have been able to come to terms with my loss of function over time. My trauma has not been the condition itself but more the way the diagnosis was handled, and the binary way in which the Navy handled my release. The disability or diabetes cause me no bitterness at all. Sometimes, I even feel fortunate that it is me that has these conditions as opposed to someone who is more predisposed to asking why.

I don't handle pity well. I'm not interested in it. It's a wasted emotion that doesn't serve the receiver or the giver of it. The giver can't change the situation and as for the receiver, I've lived perfectly well without the pity. It's a complete waste of time.

One of the things that has been said to me on more than one occasion, when I was using sticks and since I've been in a chair has been, "The trouble with you Ian is that nobody sees you as being disabled." What on earth does that mean? I have no idea how to interpret that, which way to take it. I'm guessing the people that say it think that they are giving me some sort of compliment. I mean. after all, who would want to be disabled? So if I'm creating a sense that I'm not actually disabled, although I obviously am, then maybe people see that as positive. Actually, it's a slap in the face because it ignores who I am. I'm not trying to be not disabled and I'm really comfortable with who I am. I'm not hiding anything or trying to be someone that I'm not. I'm certainly not going to be making a song and dance how difficult things can be for me. It ignores the struggles that I have every time I try to use a lift at work but people have left boxes in there. It ignores the fact that unless there are specific disabled toilets in the building, I can't take a shit. This is a basic human need yet we still don't provide this provision in as many places as we should. It ignores how I struggle to put my socks on every morning. It doesn't recognise that I can't roll over in bed without the use of a bedside accessory. It fails to recognise that sitting in a wheelchair has put enormous pressure on my bladder, making my urgency to pee a real problem that I need to take tablets for. If people don't see me as being disabled, I'm really not sure what I'm meant to do.

I've also had people say to me, "You're so brave, how do you do it? If I was like you, I'd top myself."

What on earth do you say to that?

Whilst disability takes an awful lot away, I strongly believe that it compensates in many other ways. People with disabilities are, without doubt, some of the most resilient people that I know. They do not give up, in many cases they have had to fight for every concession, every benefit and to be treated equally.

By far the biggest thing that I struggle with is anxiety. A fear of being compromised by my lack of strength and mobility. I talked earlier about the relative ease of my decision to start to use a wheelchair to play cricket. Up until 2013, I didn't really use a wheelchair in everyday life. I wanted to try and stay mobile and on my feet for as long as I could. But there is a trade-off. As my strength deteriorated I became more and more tired, so whilst I was still walking about using sticks, I was permanently knackered. That started to impact on work. Fatigue from the disability, coupled with a fatigue from diabetes makes life a bit of a struggle. I've always taken the view that people don't want to hear about your pain, your tiredness or your struggles. If they are interested, they'll ask. My view is that everybody is fighting their own battle in life in one way or another, so I'm not going to burden anyone with my particular battles if I can deal with them myself. However, sometimes, at the end of the day, I'm trashed. I'll often grab an afternoon nap when I can, recharge the batteries and go again. Having the flexibility to be able to do this is invaluable to me and keeps me working full-time.

When I was still walking, I'd spend my time on my feet constantly looking at the floor; trying to identify trip hazards before they found me. If I was presenting, I'd always arrive well in advance so that I could see where the wires were on the floor, so that I could either move them out of the way or work out a path to the lectern that avoided them.

One of my biggest fears on a daily basis when I worked at Marks' was to be carrying a tray of food across the dining hall and tripping over in full sight of everyone. Thankfully, it never happened. My degree of foot drop and lack of strength in my calves and quads made the fear of falling and tripping almost paralysing, and so my eventual move to a Powerchair was a huge psychological step and a relief. I am less tired for longer, now that I am using the chair, which means that I can be more productive but the downside is that the muscles that I used when I was walking, even with sticks, are now being used less and therefore get weaker. The frustration is that with this disease I just can't win.

There is sometimes a misconception, with me at least, that CMT just affects the legs; it doesn't. There are many different types of CMT, this isn't meant to be a medical book so I won't go into all of them but the type that I am supposed to have, affects the peripheral nerves in the extremities, so feet and hands. I say 'supposed to have' because I was diagnosed in 1992 with Type 1a but in January 2020, I received a letter from my Neurological Consultant to say that my DNA cannot confirm that diagnosis to be accurate. So as I write, I can't actually say for definite what it is exactly that cause my problems.

The receipt of this news messed with my head. When I was diagnosed in 1993 it provided answers. I was able to explain to Dad what I had been told and therefore provide him with some answers too. Over the years I've been able to explain to people what the problem is, how it affects me and the likely prognosis. That clarity has now been taken away – I don't know officially what is wrong with me or the impact, if any, that it will have on my children. Everything that I thought I knew is now in doubt. Obviously, what isn't in doubt is my functional limitation. There must be a reason why my strength and balance are so depleted. More than ever, I am convinced the drugs given to me in the Gulf have played a part in things.

My fingers, hands, wrists, forearms and deltoids have lost so much strength. My shoulders are still pretty good and I really hope that remains the case. I struggle to tie shoelaces, to fasten buttons and to use knives and forks; my grip is pathetic. Speaking of grip, how do you react when someone shakes your hand deliberately firm, in a way that you feel as if they are trying to crush your hand? I hate it, always have. What are they trying to prove?

I'm not a fan of a limp handshake either but there is a middle ground. I now struggle to offer a decent handshake in the way that I used to because my grip has deserted me and I've lost count of the times that upon shaking someone's hand, I've been called limp wrist or lettuce wrist; or received the smug smile from someone who recognises that they have a stronger handshake than I have.

It's as if they think that they have achieved some sort of initial victory over you and that you should feel immediately inferior because they can squeeze quite hard.

One of the biggest anxieties that I have is that everybody always comes to ours for parties and the like. Whilst this makes things much easier for Jo and me on a practical level, in that I am in a familiar place and I am comfortable and if I fall, then at least I am at home; it creates a problem on another level. Our friends always end up travelling to ours and I feel bad that Jo does all the catering and sorting out beforehand if we have guests coming over. Secondly, it's only natural for others to want to host parties and gatherings at their house from time to time but this causes issues for me. The biggest issue being the fact that only some of our friends have toilets downstairs.

An example of the anxieties I have was when our friends Tim and Tracey had invited us all over for a cheese and wine evening. The sort of evening that ordinarily I would love and Tim couldn't wait to have us all over as they'd done a lot of work to the house and they wanted to show it off. I was anxious all day; I knew that whatever I drank I would need to be careful because their toilet was upstairs and there was no way that I would be making it. In the past, Tim had set up a portaloo in his garage which I accessed via the back garden but that just wasn't going to work on this particular evening because of the ice outside. Besides which, I now really struggled with the size of the step from his backdoor down to the path in the garden. On top of that, I just hated the fact that the next morning he had the unenviable task of washing away my piss from the night before. The whole situation was just uncomfortable. Tim feels awful that they haven't got a downstairs toilet and I feel awful that he needs to clean my piss up in the mornings. It's either that or I disappear round the back of his house and piss on his fence – the whole thing is just awkward. I don't like it and it makes me feel very uncomfortable.

But what do we do? We can't expect everyone to keep coming round to ours, and then us declining their offer of hospitality when it is offered. As I said, I'd been anxious all day about the toilet situation and then on top of that we had an icy driveway to negotiate. The whole event filled me with dread and yet all I wanted to do was sit and have a drink with our mates.

Jo was working the next day and so we were never going to be staying late. We figured that if I went to the toilet before we left, then I should be OK for a few hours until it was time to leave. And so it proved, we left at about 9:30, by which time I was bursting. But the whole fun of the evening was lost on me, all the while I was watching what I was drinking. I was sat in the dining room because the chairs were easy for me to get out of but most of the fellas gravitated towards the lounge where the chairs are naturally softer and more difficult for me to get out of, so I was never going to sit in there.

I was sad to leave but by the same token, glad to be back home. A day's worth of anxiety and worry about the evening had left me shattered and not much fun, and I was asleep before Jo.

The whole situation frustrates the hell out of me. I'm sure people look at me and think, how on earth can he travel all over the world with work but struggle so much at home?

That was a typical situation a few years ago. Now, I very rarely go out during the winter and definitely not when the snow and ice is about. I'm scared to leave the house in case I slip and injure myself. I hate it. I hate the impact that it has on me and the family. If I fall, I cannot get myself up. If I damage either of my arms or my hands, then I am completely stuffed because I use them for everything. Some may view my approach as being over-cautious but then, they don't know me like I do. You hear so often about older people being isolated during the winter – that's exactly how I feel when I'm at home on my own during the winter.

I can't remember the last time I went to a friend's house and went inside. As my legs have deteriorated and I can't manage the smallest steps or to walk without balancing on something, furniture surfing, it's difficult to get into other people's houses, and their homes are not set up for a wheelchair as ours is.

It feels as if my world is getting smaller. I stick to places where I know I'm going to be safe and independent. Strangely, because I have my routine, I'm comfortable travelling to London and going to Lord's. It really isn't a problem because the hotel where I stay is accessible and I can get to the office easily. I can scoot around St John's Wood and all the taxis have ramps if I need to go further afield. I don't use the tube because I'm not familiar with which tube stops have lifts.

When I travel abroad with work, it is relatively easy for me. Airports are accessible and we stay in hotels when we get to our destination and for the most part, the hotels are fine. There are plenty of people about, to give me a hand if needed. Some of these trips are not without difficulty and I have made reference to some of my hotel nightmares elsewhere in the book.

By far, the hardest part of travelling is the flight for me. Economy Class seats are just not designed for people with physical disability. I have been fortunate in that ECB have allowed me to travel business class, it has made such a difference. It's the difference between being helpless and dependent on others and retaining dignity and independence.

I've had some awful experiences, being a disabled person, travelling abroad. Every time a plane reaches its destination, the cabin crew come round to tell the disabled passengers to stay in their seats until the rest of the passengers have cleared the plane. If the plane has come to a standstill on the tarmac, rather than next to an airbridge at the terminal building, you have to wait until a vehicle with a lift platform on it arrives to get you off the plane – and that's if you are lucky. On many occasions I've been carried down aircraft steps by ground crew. Contrary to my earlier point about travelling with dignity, quite often any dignity retained can soon be lost. Once off the plane, you get put into a wheelchair/ assisted passenger holding area. No wandering around the duty free or bars and restaurants for those needing assistance. When I've travelled business class, I've been wheeled into the lounge, which is nice but often the wheelchair is not one that you can propel yourself, so once your porter has left to go and help others, you are stuck where you are left. You can see the beautiful buffet and the fridge full of cold beer but you can't actually get to it. Neither can you get to the toilet.

I'm sad to say that the experience in UK airports is often the worst. On each flight there may be two or three wheelchair users or passengers requiring assistance. After you've waited for all the other passengers to leave the plane, you might still be waiting for the wheelchair to take to you baggage reclaim to arrive. It could be up to an hour after the aircraft has touched down before you get off the plane. Quite often, there is only one person to push two or three wheelchairs. So, one at a time, we get taken up the airbridge and into the terminal building and then we have to wait while he/she goes back to the aircraft to wheel someone else up. Once the wheelchairs (as we are known and referred to) are all inside the terminal building, we are taken, two at a time (one pushed and one pulled and one left behind), through to Passport Control and on to baggage reclaim. Often, we get asked to transfer from a manual wheelchair into a different wheelchair or one of the buggies that you see meandering about the terminal buildings. This is a nightmare for me. Invariably, the wheelchair seats are low and I really struggle to get out of them. After a long-haul flight, I'm tired, weak and stiff and such a transfer is really difficult. I need help. Apparently some wheelchairs have to stay "airside" so they need to use another wheelchair to access the rest of the terminal building. For me, it is an unnecessary hassle which makes the whole experience more stressful. If I happen to be the "wheelchair" that is left behind whilst the Porter takes the first two through, the changing of the wheelchair scenario is the straw that breaks the back of my patience. Arriving at a UK airport as a wheelchair user is one of the very few experiences in life where I actually feel both vulnerable and very second-class.

Bobby Denning and I at the opening ceremony of the 1st Blind Cricket T20 World Cup in Bangalore

Mum & Dad

Me with the Cricket World Cup 2019

Jo and I at Buckingham Palace in 2006. The England Team had just been presented with honours following their Ashes victory the previous summer. We were introduced to the Queen and the Duke of Edinburgh but I remember being more in awe meeting Freddie Flintoff and KP.

Playing a pull shot at Loughborough in 2009

Celebrating England winning the World Cup at Lord's in 2019. What a day.

Conor and I at Dubai international Cricket Stadium in 2016.

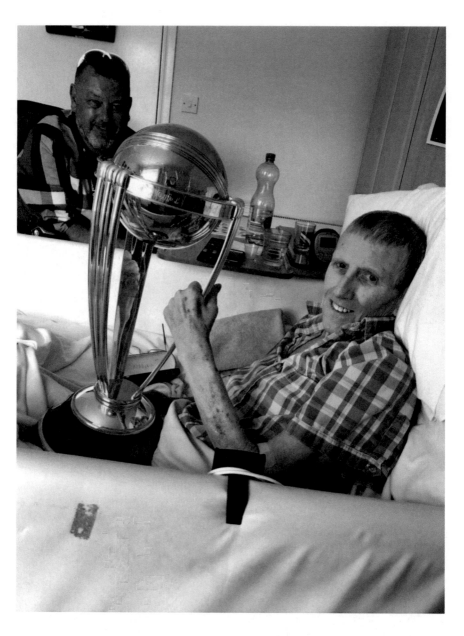

I was able to take the cricket World Cup to show Dad in his nursing home. He was so so weak at this point he couldn't lift it.

Mum holding Conor, and her father, Harold Newbury. A hero, an inspiration and greatly missed.

The only chance I got to bat at Lord's was in the Indoor Centre. I hope to see that change for future generations of disabled players.

Jo and I at Buckingham Palace in 2018. In the afternoon we were at a Garden Party with the Queen and other members of the Royal Family...

.......and in the evening I met the King at Lord's!! They say it's best not to meet
your hero's. In my case it was an absolute privilege and one of the highlights of my life.
I've been in awe of Sir Viv Richards since I was a child and I felt like a giddy kid here.

With members of the World Cup winning England Physical Disability Cricket Team following a reception at No.10. From L-R Qasim Ali (Head Coach), Matt Askin, Iain Nairn MBE, Dan Reynaldo and Fred Bridges.

One of the joys of touring is enjoying different experiences. This is me with a lion cub at a sanctuary near Kimberley in 2011. As I remember, getting out of the chair, that had sunk into the grass, was a less enjoyable experience.

Rub-a-Dub-Dub – Stranded in a Tub

I've had some horrendous and some hilarious experiences as a result of this disability. I've spoken before about nervousness and anxiety when I have to venture into unknown territory and it's largely because of traumatic past experience. I've made changes to my lifestyle to limit the chance for misfortune to find me when I'm out and about. For example, I don't go out drinking in unfamiliar places unless I know that I'm with people who I'm confident have my back. I can't remember the last time that I was so drunk that I couldn't look after myself but then that might also be a sign of getting old.

One of the adaptations that we needed to pay for at home was to have our bathroom converted to a wet room. We used to have a bath with a shower over it. As time went on, standing in the bath to shower, even with a mat, was becoming more and more potentially dangerous for me, and the fear of slipping just took away any enjoyment that I took from showering. I started to have a bath on a daily basis instead and for a few years, this worked well. I figured out a way of getting in and out of the bath that was safe for me but over time, as my strength deteriorated, this became harder and harder.

One morning in 2014, I had a nightmare. I had a Chiropodist appointment, so I had a bath first thing in the morning to clean my feet. Conor wanted me to write a cheque for his dinner money for school which I clearly couldn't do whilst in the bath. As I mentioned earlier, I got out of the bath in a certain way. It involved using my shoulders to lift myself onto the side of the bath. It all needed to be done in one movement and it took quite a bit out of me. If I didn't get it right, then there was not enough strength left in my arms to try again for quite a while.

Try as I might, I just couldn't get out of the bath. The bath water had drained and I was naked in an empty bath, just getting colder. I did not have the power to lift myself out and I couldn't get any traction with my feet or legs because the bath was so slippery. Joanna had left for work and it was just me, 13-year-old Conor and 9-year-old Ciara in the house, just the worst scenario. I felt helpless and very vulnerable because I didn't know how I was going to get out of the bath. Conor just wanted to get out of the door to go and meet his mates and go to school. It must have been awful for him to see his dad struggling in such a way. I dried my hands and tried to write his cheque but my arms and hands were so fatigued that I could hardly hold the pen. The ink barely made a mark on the cheque.

I eventually managed to get out of the bath but it took me forever to get changed. I heard Conor tell Ciara that if I fell, she had to call Joanna. I had to get Ciara to tie my shoelaces as I didn't have the strength in my fingers for the small intricate movements required. I felt awful, so dependent on others for the most basic things in life. I hated that my kids should see me like this.

When we talk about disability, these are the things that people don't see.

On another occasion, I stayed in the Holiday Inn in Bristol prior to a disability cricket meeting at the County Ground at Neville Road. Again, I had a bath in the morning before breakfast because I didn't want to risk slipping in the shower. It took me three quarters of an hour trying to get out of the bath. I ended up getting my head and shoulders over the side and using gravity to get onto the floor and for my legs to follow. I then needed to crawl from the bathroom back towards the bed so that I could haul myself up. I missed breakfast. I was exhausted before the day had begun, and I had a three and a half-hour drive back home after the meeting.

This brings me on to the subject of accessible bathrooms in hotels – there is another book I could write on the topic. They range from the sublime to the ridiculous and I have had some absolute nightmares. I don't class myself as an accessibility expert, although I do have some experience in the area. It is quite obvious when you check into a hotel whether they give a damn or whether they are doing the bare minimum to be compliant. In most cases, a guest who requests an accessible room will be a wheelchair user or have mobility issues and/or a weakness in the legs. Therefore, it would help if the bed was at least at the height that would enable easy transfer from a wheelchair, and not be a foot off the ground or so high that we can't get our legs on.

Make sure the toilet is raised a bit higher than normal and has bars on either side, for the user to push up and use for leverage.

And my biggest bugbear?... Simply provide a wet room. I can't walk, so a shower with a handrail that's over a bath is absolutely useless to me.

It's really not that difficult when you think about it.

Disability Cricket and Cricketers

Without doubt, the last 20 years have been the steepest learning curve and the best time of my life. This is due to the people whom I have met through work, and the cricketers with different impairments whom our program has given opportunities to.

The game has changed beyond recognition from what I first got involved in in 2000. Cricket is not a Paralympic sport and therefore it does not enjoy the exposure that those sports under the Paralympic umbrella enjoy. Disability Cricket does not receive UK Sport funding and our national players are not contracted.

Having said that, I believe we offer an opportunity for anybody, with any disability to access our sport at a level that is appropriate for them. I am able to say, confidently, that disability cricket changes lives. I know this because I'm proof of it.

My story is one amongst hundreds of different backstories amongst our players. I have seen players with Learning Disability grow from boys into adults as a result of being away from home and on tour with us. There are many similar tales told by our blind cricketers about how involvement in cricket gave them the confidence to live an independent life. Disability cricket has given so many people the opportunity to continue to enjoy their sport of choice and to develop their own unique skills.

Blind Cricket is the most amazing sport that I think you could ever watch. It is simply amazing to watch how these visually impaired cricketers play the game. One of the first successes that I had when I joined ECB was changing the culture within the England Blind team setup. and I developed a real close relationship with many of the players who had been wanting a change for a long time.

Over time, the players in all of our squads have become more professional in their approach to the game. They see themselves as elite cricketers who need to live and behave like athletes, and this is reflected whenever they have media exposure or when they interact with young disabled people who become inspired by what our players have achieved. The change in culture and approach opened up doors for the squads to interact with the senior men's team. There is a respect shown and players from the senior squads recognise the disabled players as international cricketers, and they are sometimes in awe of what our players achieve whilst adapting to their impairment.

The best example of this that I can give is when England's World Cup-winning captain, Eoin Morgan, came to meet some of our Blind Cricketers at the indoor school at Lord's. The idea was for Eoin to experience batting as a visually impaired cricketer. To do this, he was asked to wear glasses that simulated the impact of different visual impairment. So, one pair simulated tunnel vision, whereby the glasses were blacked out except for a very small gap, perhaps the size of a pinhead, through which the batsman can see. Another pair were foggy with all-round visual restriction, and another pair were completely blacked so he couldn't see a thing.

Eoin faced our England blind team bowlers wearing each set of glasses and had mixed success in striking the ball. The session was scheduled for about 45 minutes but Morgan stayed much longer. He was so engaged, and our blind cricketers loved having him show so much interest in their game. At the end of the session, the Blind players thanked him for giving his time and being so engaged. Clearly impressed by the skill of the blind players, Eoin Morgan thanked them for showing him a side of the game that he had not previously been aware of.

Experiences like that are priceless and are one of the things that alignment of the disabled game with ECB has been able to deliver.

One of the first successes that I had in my role was establishing the Outstanding Service to Disability Cricket Award as part of the annual NATWEST-sponsored OSCA's. Through this award, I was able to ensure that those volunteers who got disability cricket started across each impairment group could be recognised, by ECB, for the contribution that they had made to the game.

Another award that I was able to introduce was the England Disabled Player of the Year. This award recognised the performance of one of our national squad players who had excelled during international disability cricket fixtures over the course of the year.

The award used to be presented at a dinner in the Long Room at Lord's alongside the England Men's and Women's Players of the Year. Each year I would go up on stage and get interviewed by the host, usually Nasser Hussain, about the disability team's performances over the previous year and then talk about the winner of the award. I loved these nights, mixing with the men's and women's teams and really starting to feel as if disability cricket was starting to be taken seriously. One time I came down off the stage and Andy Flower stopped me on the way back to my table and told me I had spoken really well. I was made up with that. Andy was someone to whom I really looked up to. We'd never spoken at that point and I was made up just to be in the same room as him. Over the years I've had the opportunity to spend time with Andy and he's every bit the class act I thought he was, a top man.

As I watched our disabled players receive their award each year, I could only imagine how amazing they must feel. Being recognised in the same place, at the same time, as your hero in the senior teams. What an honour.

Over the years, interaction between the disability squads and the senior squads has been limited, mainly because of the touring schedules of the squads. But when it does take place, it's rewarding and magical for everyone involved.

One of the best experiences was in 2017 when Andrew Strauss, Managing Director of England Cricket at the time, called me when I was on tour with the Blind Team in India. He said that he had organised an event where every living player, male or female, that had represented England, was being invited to Lord's to receive a personalised cap. It was an initiative aimed at recognising the history of the sport in England and connecting past generations of England cricketers with the current England players. Straussy also wanted our disability teams represented at the event.

So, one night in February 2017, I hosted a table in the Nursery Pavilion at Lord's during what must have been the biggest gathering of England cricketers ever assembled. I was joined by Iain Nairn, captain of the Physical Disability team, Umesh Valjee, Captain of the Deaf Team, Chris Edwards, captain of the Learning Disability Team and Matt Dean and Luke Sugg who were the captains of the ODI and T20 Blind Teams.

This was a most special evening. It was such a privilege to be in the same room as these guys. It really was the living history of the English game – and me. I never had the opportunity to pull on an England shirt. I hadn't felt the pride of representing England on a cricket field at home or abroad. But what I had done was play a large part in ensuring that players sitting around me at our table were recognised for their achievements on the field in an England shirt. I'd put them on the map. As I sat there, I still felt like a gate-crasher, this was a night for the players and I really couldn't believe that I'd been invited.

It was really difficult to not act like a complete cricket tragic getting photos and autographs. As the night went on, you could see all these former brothers-in-arms getting together and reminiscing over old times. It was magical, a real who's who of English cricket. We spent time with Joe Root, David Lloyd and the late Bob Willis. The highlight for me was meeting Sir Ian Botham and hearing him tell Nairny that he should stop smoking.

Every now and again the job gives me an opportunity or an experience that I will remember for the rest of my life. That night was certainly one of them.

Having our disabled players recognised as England representatives in the same way that Sir Alastair Cook, Sir Andrew Strauss, David Gower and Sir Ian Botham have been recognised was a real proud moment.

Whilst disability cricket has moved a long way, not just in the UK but globally too, we still have some way to go before real equity is achieved. The disabled game has to face some challenges.

I have a real fear for the future of Deaf Cricket. Technology and medical science is moving on all of the time. Youngsters with hearing impairments in countries like the UK, Australia and possibly South Africa are being fitted with cochlea implants at a young age. As a result of this, they are living a very different life to the older generation of hearing-impaired people who never had access to such technology.

Deaflympic rules state that competitors must remove hearing aids and cochlea implants before competing. In cricket, this means that no player can cross the boundary onto the playing area wearing a hearing aid or a cochlea implant. This creates a level playing field for those who are completely deaf and for whom such devices do not work.

The rule itself makes sense and is understandable. However, I feel that without some sort of flexibility we are going to hit a problem down the line. This is because the youngsters who have devices fitted at a young age essentially grow up in a mainstream society and environment. They get their first taste of cricket in the same way that any other youngster does and if they enjoy the sport, they will progress to their local club. They will develop and get better and eventually move into senior cricket, all without having to remove their hearing aid. They then might become aware of international deaf cricket and find that they are good enough to get involved in the national squad setup, only to be told that they have to remove their hearing aids or cochlea implant in order to play. This is something that they never needed to have done before and changes their world considerably. Why would any youngster consider it when they have played regular club cricket all of their lives with no problem at all?

This issue will become more and more prevalent as time goes on. Of course, the challenge will be how to create a level playing field because access to such technology is not as easy in countries like India, Pakistan and Bangladesh. So, the development of the sport in those countries will continue as it has done, with no appetite for change.

Another challenge that faces all of the different impairment groups, particularly in the UK, is that we are fishing in a relatively small pond for our talent. People with a disability in the UK have options and aspirations. They don't have to settle for what is presented to them. A talented disabled sportsman or woman has the choice of numerous different sports to get involved in, some of which have a Paralympic pathway and UK Sport funding. At the moment, cricket does not offer this.

The situation in South East Asia and the Indian subcontinent is very different. Cricket is THE sport. It is a religion in that part of the world and youngsters aspire to be like their heroes in our sport. Cricket gets the first pick of the talent and there are thousands to choose from. Sure, there are other sports available, but cricket is the one that they all want to succeed in. Culturally, disabled people are treated very differently in that part of the world, and being a member of the Indian or Pakistani national disability sides brings payment and a chance to contribute to the family alongside huge self-esteem and local profile within the community.

If England and Australia are ever going to compete consistently with India and Pakistan in Blind and Deaf cricket in particular, there needs to be changes in our approach to disability cricket because at the moment we can't compete against guys who are essentially professional players, training full-time and taking a wage.

What me and my team at ECB are endeavouring to achieve in England and Wales is for cricket to be seen as a credible disability sport. We need to ensure that a disabled youngster who enjoys our sport decides to stick with it and pursue his or her sporting ambitions in cricket rather than switching to a Paralympic sport.

The challenge is that cricket cannot yet offer the funding to allow our disabled talent to train full-time, and as I mentioned earlier, there are many sports for disabled people to access in the UK. Therefore, we need to make what we offer, top class, in terms of access to elite-level coaching, world class facilities and science and medical support when needed. I am sure that cricket can be the number one dual-career disability sport in the UK. By dual career, I mean that players can achieve the sporting aspirations as well as their professional career goals. It doesn't need to be one or the other.

Touring

One of the best parts of my role at ECB has been accompanying our National Disability Squads on overseas tours and to World Cups. I've been fortunate to have been on 18 or 19 trips now, and have experienced every emotion going as I've watched the performances of our teams, and more importantly, the growth of our players and those of our opponents. I've been able to make friends (and probably some enemies) all over the world.

There are stories to be told from each trip abroad. The mix of performance, banter and camaraderie is potent and I have found it to be like a drug. Getting back to the everyday of being at home after two or three weeks on a massive high is a huge downer, and I still don't think I manage it as well as I could.

Things are much easier for me now as Bradders takes on much more of the logistical arrangements as our Operations Manager, but before he came in full-time, I would be a world away in the lead up to departure. Our house would resemble a warehouse with boxes of kit all over the place. Again Joanna has been a saint over the years for putting up with this. As we'd get about two weeks away from departure, I could feel myself entering a bit of a pre-tour bubble. My mind would be thinking about nothing else other than the trip ahead. I wanted to leave nothing to chance, particularly around eligibility of our players, Visas and passports and air tickets. Baggage Allowance was always a concern, I can't think of many trips where one player, or maybe more, wasn't unpacking and repacking before checking in.

I remember briefing our Blind Squad upon arriving in Sydney in 2008 to keep wise cracks to a minimum as we passed through Australian Immigration and not to react to any comments we might receive. Arriving in Australia as an England Cricket Team, emblazoned in team tracksuits and large sponsor-branded cricket bags – you are an obvious target for some sort of comment from the locals who are only too pleased to let you know that you're gonna get stuffed. They seem unable to refer to us as English – it's either 'Bloody Poms' or 'Pommy Baaastards'.

Anyway, one by one, we passed through immigration having answered some standard questions. Just as I thought all was going swimmingly, I overheard the following exchange between one of our players and an Aussie Immigration Officer:

Officer – "Welcome to Australia, how long are you staying?"
Player – "Two weeks, should be long enough to beat your lot."
Officer – "Any criminal record back home?"
Player – "Didn't think we needed one to get in here anymore."

Not surprisingly, our player ended up emptying his bags at customs so that Australian Immigration could check that there was no soil on his cricket boots as importing plants or soil into Australia could damage their unique eco-system.

On another occasion, I was flying back from Australia with our Deaf Squad. We flew home via Singapore and there was time for another Martin wheelchair drama. We had a couple of hours to wait for our connecting flight to London and Peter Dixon, our Team Manager, took control of pushing me in an airport wheelchair to the departure gate. Spirits were high, maybe a couple of cans of beer had been enjoyed. We proceeded through terminal building towards our destination and used one of those travelator walkways, the things that look like escalators but are flat on the ground. Now, Peter is a big bloke and as we proceeded down the travelator, I was conscious that his large, bounding, stride coupled with the speed of the travelator meant that I was being pushed at a fair speed. This was great until the end of the walkway was in sight. There was a slight lip where the travelator ended and the concourse began, and I was heading towards it at a rate of knots. I knew that if the front wheels of the wheelchair hit the lip at this speed, there was likely to be carnage that followed. Peter, meanwhile, was unaware of the impending disaster, he was busy talking to some of the others as I was imploring him to slow down.

Too late…

As the casters on the front of the wheelchair hit the lip, I was catapulted forward and landed in a heap on the floor. The wheelchair and Peter followed and were now blocking the exit at the end of the Travelator. There were cricket bags and Deaf cricketers all piled up – every one of us in stitches at what had happened. There were looks of disgust from passengers travelling in the opposite direction. Nobody rushed to help. I don't know how long we were on the floor for but it was quite a while. We couldn't move for laughing – arms and legs everywhere. Absolute carnage. Whoever was monitoring the Terminal CCTV that night must have had a right laugh.

There are stories like this from every tour; I reckon there are enough for at least one more book. Whilst there are countless laughs on tour, it is also a pretty serious business. As a management group we are looking after the welfare of our players, all of whom are classed as vulnerable adults, some are under 18 and are covered by safeguarding rules. We are also representing ECB and therefore our nation, which whilst invokes immense pride, also carries with it responsibilities that club touring sides don't have.

There are any number of functions to attend, arranged by our hosts or by the British High Commission in the area that we are visiting. I mostly enjoy these events as you get a real insight into the work that the foreign office do to develop trade relations and further British interests in different countries. The British diplomatic offices are usually pretty impressive and we get very well-looked after. In many cases, the Ambassador and his or her staff will come and watch the teams play, and it's great to have some British support whilst we are abroad.

But of course, the best thing about touring is the people that you encounter. Someone once said to me that when you think about all the best experiences that you have in your life – in the vast majority of cases you are never on your own, other people are with you. I have found this to be so true. Being around cricket people, in different cricket environments all over the world have been some of the best times of my life, and these experiences have been shared with some great people.

It is this that makes touring so addictive, you can never have enough good times.

Because the players in our National Disability Squads are not contracted or professional players, they need to take time off work or university to enable them to represent their country. Therefore, our tours are much shorter than the National men's and women's teams. We have to find the balance between making the trips worthwhile in terms of the amount of cricket that is played and looking after the players from a welfare and fitness perspective. There can be a lot of cricket played in a short period of time with not much downtime for players or staff. A typical matchday will start with an alarm around 6:30–7 am. Breakfast between seven and eight am. Transport to the ground at 8:30. Warm Ups. Game start at 10:30–11 am. Game finish around 4–4:30. Warm Downs, presentations, shower and change, transport back to the hotel. Dinner, Team Meeting 8–8:30 pm. Managers will then get together and review the day and plan for the next day. Everything should be finished by 10 pm. Then it's off to bed, ready to do it all again tomorrow if there is another game. It can be a bit like Groundhog Day. This all assumes that the day has been straightforward with no issues on or off the pitch. You could easily have to add in meetings with umpires and match referees, there could be player welfare issues, the Physio will need time to work on aches and strains and the Performance Analyst will want to review and provide insight from the day's game.

But even when you are most tired, you have to remember that so many people would jump at the chance to do what we do – the experience is to be enjoyed and savoured; for me it is the best part of my job.

Some of the best and happiest times of my life have been spent with our disability squads on tour. Winning and losing games of cricket, the intensity of competition and the chance to sit down and enjoy a beer in the sun afterwards is magical. I've spent hours in the company of amazing people during times when I've not been feeling so great, and the banter and laughs we've had have been priceless.

Mr Ian's Toilet Problem

In 2017, I had been in Bangladesh for a meeting and flew into Dubai for another meeting before heading home. It was a 5-hour flight from Dhaka to Dubai and upon arrival at the hotel, I needed the toilet as a matter of urgency. I got to my room, got into the "accessible" bathroom and sat on the lower-than-average toilet. Safe in the knowledge that I'd avoided what would have been a fairly catastrophic entrance to my new room had I not made it to the loo, I checked out how I was going to get off the toilet. There was a handrail. Great. However, it was that far away that even with my right arm fully outstretched, I couldn't wrap my fingers around it. It seemed as if they'd located it equidistant between the toilet and the shower, so as to render it entirely useless for either.

I shifted my position on the seat and lent further over to see if I could get both hands on it. I nearly fell off the toilet so that wasn't going to work. On my left-hand side was a sink unit, but as I was sitting down, the top of the unit was above my shoulders, so pushing down with my hands to raise me from the toilet wasn't going to work. Then, to my relief, they'd thought of everything. In the event that a disabled person found their accessible bathroom completely useless, they'd installed a phone.

It wasn't the ideal conversation with concierge or the front desk, but after 20 minutes trying to figure out how to get off the bog without ending up on the floor with my trousers around my ankles, needs must.

I lifted the receiver to be greeted by… absolutely nothing. A whole load of dead line.

Thankfully, in a moment of inspiration, I realised that my mobile phone was in my trouser pocket. So, onto the Wi-Fi, google the hotel, find the number for the front desk and dial it. So the call goes via satellite to the UK, then gets relayed back from UK to the front desk in Dubai where I get to speak to the same charming lady who checked me in not half an hour earlier. "Hi, it's Mr Martin in Room 624, I have a slight problem in that I am disabled and I can't get off the toilet." Really not what you want to be saying but it was a desperate situation.

"Hello Mr Ian, sorry what is wrong with the toilet?"

"It's Mr Martin and there's nothing wrong with the toilet other than the fact that I can't get off it."

"OK Mr Ian, are you ok?"

"No, I'm disabled, and I can't get off the toilet."

"Oh OK, Mr Ian, I'll send somebody now".

Stay calm Ian, help is on its way I thought.

Twenty minutes later, nobody had arrived so I rang again. Ten minutes later there's a knock on my door.

"Come in!" I shout.

"Can you open the door?" comes the reply.

"No, I'm stuck on the toilet."

"Sorry, what is wrong with the toilet?"

"There's nothing wrong with the fucking toilet, I just need to get off it, I need help."

I'm beginning to lose the plot by this stage. I'd been in their hotel for over an hour and spent the whole time on the shitter.

"OK Mr Ian, I'll get my friend." He replies.

Brilliant! I thought, my plight is now becoming a spectator event.

What seemed like ages but was probably only five minutes later, two men, armed with a plunger and a plumber's tool kit, entered my room and found me in the bathroom.

"Sorry, Mr Ian. We didn't understand, now what is wrong with the toilet?"

I wanted to cry. All I wanted was to go and lie down on the bed and have an overpriced beer from the mini bar.

They lifted me off the loo. I pulled up my pants and said thanks.

All because whoever fitted the hand rail had no idea about how it might actually be used.

ICC World Cup Final 2015

I'd been in Melbourne for a Learning Disability Ashes series which we had won 5-1. I'd arranged to stay on for a few days extra to attend the World Cup Final being held at the MCG. So after the lads had flown home the day before, I woke up on 26th March, knowing that I had nothing to do and nowhere to go. It was brilliant.

That said, I felt a little isolated and perhaps vulnerable as a disabled guy on my own, 10000 miles away from home. I knew that if something went horribly wrong, then I had people around upon whom I could call for help but the purpose of this for me was to see how I coped. Was I going to stay in the hotel or was I going to get out and about and front up to whatever Melbourne had to challenge the disabled person with?

I needn't be worried. Melbourne was very accessible to me and my scooter. I spent hours going around the MCG and up and down the South Bank, as well as getting into Bourke Street and the little alley ways that are Melbourne's hidden gems. So much of it was familiar to me and brought back memories of when we did Wanted Down Under. The only thing missing was Jo, she'd have loved just wandering around with nowhere in particular to be.

I spent the Saturday morning down at the G, watching the preparation for the World Cup final the next day. I bumped into Nasser Hussain who came over to congratulate me on our series win. He was really genuine too; said he'd seen the tweets and social media stuff and was genuinely pleased that we'd won. He's a lovely guy from the experience that I have of him and it was great that he took the time out to come and say hello. I also saw Adam Mountford, the TMS producer who also congratulated me on the series win.

The extra days I had allowed me to catch up with some old friends whose company I had enjoyed on previous trips Down Under and elsewhere. On Thursday night, I went out with some guys who do/did work for Cricket Australia and Cricket Victoria.

Annie Hateley organised the dinner and we went to Rosetta on the South Bank, a beautiful Italian restaurant. Annie had worked for CV for years and was the heart and soul behind CV's community engagement programme. She makes a lot of stuff happen and was behind the 2009 Tri-Series and the 2011 Deaf Ashes Series. She is really well-respected and it was sad to hear that she was feeling so disillusioned with cricket that she was looking to leave and seek pastures new. Such a shame.

Paul Montgomery was Head of Coach Education at CV. I first met him in Cape Town in 2005 when he was Head Coach of the Australian LD team. He's a great guy, always laughing and with a funny story to tell. When we were in Melbourne in 2007 doing Wanted Down Under, we went to his place for a Barbi with his family. I always try and catch up with him when I'm in Melbourne.

Neale Price is one of the best blokes you could ever meet. I first met Pricey in the Danubius hotel in London. Pete Ackerley introduced me that night as being so pissed that my legs didn't know whether they were coming or going before I'd had a drink, let alone after a skinful. Pricey is a diamond of a bloke. He used to work for CA and I worked with him on 2009 Tri-Series and the 2011 Deaf Ashes and we had some communication during the farcical 2008 Blind Ashes. Just a top man.

Bruce Nunn was Head Coach of the Australian LD team in Kimberley in 2011. Spent many an evening with him, Nev Paulsen and Greg Brown drinking a glass of red whilst talking all things cricket. Another great bloke.

Finally Kristen Beams. First met KB in 2008 when she came up to Penrith CC during the infamous Blind Ashes series in 2008 to try and figure out what on earth was going on. We've caught up regularly ever since. She was part of the team with Annie and Pricey who delivered the 2009 Tri-Series and 2011 Deaf Ashes. She played for the Essex women's team in 2013 and so we were able to catch up in London then and it was great to see her again, particularly now that she was part of the Southern Stars team and would come to England later in the year on an Ashes tour.

It was a lovely evening with lots of laughs and just great to see these guys again.

On Friday, I went out with Aaron Dragwidge from CA. Aaron picked me up and we went for a few beers at a pub in Richmond followed by a Chefs banquet at Two Fat Indians, an upmarket curry house just up from my hotel. Great meal but neither of us could finish it. Aaron is a diamond and I hope we remain friends for a long time, a real decent fella who is involved in disability cricket for all the right reasons.

Finally, on the Saturday afternoon, I got to spend a couple of hours with the best of the lot. Greg Brown. Older than my dad but as tough as old boots. Brownie played AFL for Essendon back in the '60s and was one of their directors. He is the only man to have played Premier Cricket and Football for Essendon in the same season. He was the Chairman of the Lord's Taverners Australia. The man is a colossus in every sense of the word. When he shakes your hand, its stays shook. Greg and Jill picked me up and we went to a restaurant called the Bouzy Rouge in Richmond. It was a great spot, a Spanish Tapas place where the food was delicious. We had a 12-hour slow-cooked lamb shoulder amongst other tapas and it was beautiful. Greg and I polished off a couple of bottles of Pepperjack, my new favourite Aussie Red and a great afternoon was had.

So, I awoke on the Sunday morning for the last time on that visit to Australia. I had my bags pretty much packed and I was looking forward to the World Cup Final. It was a glorious day. Aaron and Robyn's son Dene met me in reception and Robyn arrived shortly after. We loaded my bags into her car and I took a change of clothes to the ground ready for me to change into pre-flight. My ticket was for the Olympic Room, ICC hospitality and I was dressed, as requested, in business attire. I needn't have bothered. The dress code had not been adhered to by the majority.

This was another one of those days where I had to pinch myself to believe where I actually was. This was something I'd dreamed about since being a kid. The best bit of it was, I'd not had to pay a penny.

The MCG was awesome. 93,000 people were in and when Brendon McCullum, the NZ skipper, was bowled by the 3rd delivery of the match, the stadium erupted. The noise was deafening. I only knew two people in the room. Giles Clark, the ECB President and Chair of the ICC Finance committee and Steve Elworthy, ECB's Global Events Director. I was keen to speak to both. I caught up with Steve quite early on and we discussed the disability event that will run parallel to the ICC World Cup in England in 2019. I'd put a paper forward to Paul.

Downton for his thoughts before circulating it to Steve and Tom Harrison. Steve confirmed that we were committed to staging a disability event so that was good news. I eventually caught up with Giles sometime later. I discussed that I needed India or specifically BCCI to get a lot closer to disability cricket in their country – I was just getting into my flow when we got interrupted by the Head of Star TV India. Given that they and the Indian TV market virtually bankroll cricket, it was no surprise to be dropped by Giles as he headed off to look after one of ICC's main sponsors. Pleasingly, sometime later, Giles said that Shrini (Srinivasenen) had agreed to "look at" disability cricket in India. On paper, this was a step in the right direction – in reality, I probably knew what would happen.

The room was a bit of a Who's Who of Cricket. Kapil Dev, Sir Clive Lloyd, Arjuna Ranatunga and Martin Crowe to name but a few. The highlight of my afternoon came when Sachin Tendulkar entered the room. You know when Sachin is somewhere close because what seems like the whole of India descends around you, shouting "Sachin, Sachin, Sachin". Sure enough, there he was, right in the middle of a circle of bodyguards. He had come to speak to Martin Crowe who was suffering from Lymphoma and reportedly only had a few weeks to live. Sachin and Crowe spoke for about 10 minutes and then Sachin left surrounded by the chaos and adulation that announced his arrival. Fortunately for me, he walked right past me, I stuck out my hand and he shook it, looked me in the eye and said it was lovely to meet me. It was unbelievable. Not often I am awestruck these days but that was special. I looked up and saw hundreds of Indians outside, pressed up against the window of the box. This must have pissed off Clive Lloyd considerably because he was sat in an armchair next to the window, trying to watch the cricket.

The first thing that strikes you about Tendulkar is how small he is. I felt as tall as him sat on my scooter. But I don't think anything prepares you for the way that he is adored by India. I've experienced this twice now. The first time was at the MCC vs RoW game at Lord's in 2014. The noise is unbelievable. I reckon only Bradman compares with Tendulkar in terms of status and legend within cricket – so as a cricket badger/anorak, I can tell my kids of the day that I met Sachin – that's cool right?

Oh, slightly less humble than Sachin, Kapil Dev signed my programme.

A couple of hours later, I was on the plane home. I was asleep before we got airborne. I woke up, six or seven hours later, somewhere over the Indian Ocean.

Leadership

I've been fortunate through my career to have been exposed to some wonderful people on my journey and I hope I have learnt from all of them. For me, leadership is about trust and empowering your people to be the best that they can be. Nobody can do it on their own.

Disability Cricket in 2021 is unrecognisable from how it looked when I first got in involved in 2000, and certainly since I started at ECB in 2007. I started at the bottom in all of the roles that I have had since leaving school. For all of the reasons outlined earlier in this book, I have developed a drive to succeed and improve myself in each of these roles.

When I started at ECB, I was in a position of my own making to get the job, but I was helped significantly by the people who I'd been fortunate to work with, particularly at Disability Sport Wales and Conwy Council, with leaders like Jon Morgan, Michelle Daltry and Jim Jones. I learnt from all of them. When I joined ECB, I was a team of one, trying to influence a network of Cricket Development Officers/Managers and our own staff about the importance of disability inclusion. It wasn't quite an impossible job but it certainly became much easier once I was able to build a team around me.

As the team increased, my role evolved. Each newly recruited member of the team took over an element of my role and made it better. Through my voluntary roles and early years at ECB, I'd had exposure to all facets of running an area of the game from grassroots levels up to running four National Squads. Different elements of the job required different styles of leadership and I'm the first to admit that I didn't always get it right. I've come to learn through experience that getting it wrong isn't the crime, not learning from the mistake is the problem.

In my experience, the most important element of leadership is recruitment of the right people for the role. In the different roles that I have had, I sometimes think that people management experience and skill is neglected in favour of the delivery of operational outcomes or productivity and results.

In my role at the moment, I have people who are far better at delivering the component parts of the role that I inherited than I was at trying to juggle all of them. I have recruited people better than me at those roles. I see my role now as providing a strategic direction and facilitating the team to be the best that they can be in delivering the strategy.

I'm pleased to say that in the vast majority of cases, individuals who I had recruited into the disability program and who have now left, have moved into better positions elsewhere, either within the game or sport more generally. This reflects well on the disability program and ECB. At this stage of its evolution, Disability Cricket cannot offer a full career pathway. I am sure this will change as we move forward.

I have developed both as a leader and a person over the years. I've been incredibly fortunate to have worked with and observed some real quality people at work. I'd have been foolish not to have learnt from Hugh Morris, Gordon Lord, Andy Flower, Clare Connor, Paul Shaw, Bruce Cruise, Steve Elworthy, Gordon Hollins and latterly Professor John Neal. Through different courses and functions, I've been exposed to ex-special forces staff and other ex-military leadership experts such as Gemma Morgan and have taken different things from each of them.

Different environments deliver different leaders or styles of leadership. The military style of leadership that I was exposed to was very autocratic. In many ways, it needed to be because in a time of war or emergency, you need to act decisively and without question; hesitancy can cost lives. However, in a civilian environment, autocratic leadership is less likely to be successful in the long term because people need to feel involved in decision making and not just ordered about.

I recall being very autocratic when I first got involved with Blind cricket when I started at ECB. There was change needed. We had an overseas Ashes series in less than 12 months' time and I had people, whose views I trusted, telling me that change was needed. In hindsight, I went at it like a bull in a china shop. I got the changes I needed but not without a degree of pain. As Ackers would later tell me, "Sometimes when you want to make a great omelette, you have to smash a few eggs." When we won the Ashes 3-1 in Sydney 12 months later, it was worthwhile. However, If I was back in that situation again, I wonder whether I would approach it differently.

The Special Forces style of military leadership is much more aligned to my preferred style. Trust and respect is given to all members of the team. Every person's opinion is listened to and a way forward or plan is agreed. Each person is accountable for the delivery of their part of the plan.

My role as a volunteer trustee with the Lord's Taverners and with the Neuro Muscular Centre in Winsford have exposed me to more very impressive people such as Tim Luckhurst, Sandra Verkuyten and Matthew Lanham.

The one key thing that I have taken from all of them is that you are nothing without your team.

Leadership is a privilege; leaders are entrusted and are in position to guide and to serve the people whom they lead. None of us will always get it right and there will always be bumps in the road where we can learn and avoid them next time. When any of us accepts a new position, I don't believe we ever start that new role wanting to fail. So, if things don't go well, before firing your shots at the staff member, take a look in the mirror – how could YOU have helped the staff member perform better? People won't always remember how good a leader you are or are not, but they will always remember how you made them feel.

I think that sometimes my managers have struggled to understand how chronic conditions affect people. Why would they understand? If they have not been exposed to such conditions before, I can't expect them to know. Sometimes, there are no answers and no solutions other than rest. Managers, by definition, are problem solvers and want to understand why. Sometimes, with my conditions, there is no why when I'm feeling fatigued. It could be CMT, it could be diabetes and it could be a mixture of both. All I know is that I'd much rather be feeling as healthy and strong as I was when I was younger and I don't need someone trying to performance-manage my condition.

Brian Potter

In January 2017, I was in India for the Blind Cricket T20 World Cup. Getting around on my scooter wasn't easy but it was manageable with a bit of care and some help when needed. Our hosts were keen that as many people across India got to see the England team play, and our schedule was horrendous in terms of travel. Our itinerary took us from Delhi to Bangalore via Indore, Ahmedabad and Mumbai.

The logistics of travelling with 15 visually impaired cricketers, eight staff, over 40 large cricket bags, a physio table and a mobility scooter don't bear thinking about. At times our Team Manager Neil Bradshaw and I were tearing our hair out. The schedule saw our team having to travel from Delhi to Mumbai via Ahmedabad and Indore including four separate internal flights. This was a nightmare for all of us, especially with all of the luggage. Given my disability and problems boarding aircraft and getting in and out of aircraft seats, we decided that it would be better if I flew straight to our hotel in Mumbai and met the lads there when they arrived.

I arrived at Delhi airport and went to check in on my scooter, pulling my large ECB cricket bag alongside me. Nothing can prepare you for the attention you get on a mobility scooter in India. It felt like a thousand pairs of eyes were watching me as I went to check in. I could sense they were saying to each other, "Look at the mad Englishman who thinks he's going to get on a plane on his bike." As I queued to check in, people sidled up alongside me and took selfies with the scooter in the background. This happened a lot everywhere I went in India. The more confident ones would just ask, "Sir, photo with very nice bike?" How could I refuse? Being on my own, it was a bit unnerving. I didn't like the attention and it made me feel like a bit of a freak but I had absolutely no control over it.

I eventually got to check in. "Mr Martin travelling to Mumbai," I announced as I handed in my passport. "One bag and a scooter and I'll be taking the scooter to the aircraft door," I continued with the assured confidence of a seasoned traveller who had experienced airport check-in countless times before. Give me my boarding pass and I'll be on my way, no need for any assistance, I'm a very independent traveller, India doesn't faze me.

"No bike on the plane Mr Ian," said the girl on check in.

"No, no, the scooter goes in the hold," I replied.

"The bike can't go on the plane sir, not permitted on planes in India." I sensed a problem.

"How do you think I got it to India?" I asked.

This went on for about 15 minutes until a supervisor arrived and eventually sorted the issue out. Well, she sorted the check-in issue out. She disappeared before the next nightmare.

If you've ever travelled through the subcontinent, you'll be aware that security in their airports is provided by the Army and not the nice customer-facing Border Force staff that we have in the UK. I got to security and was confronted by two soldiers, each well over 6ft tall, carrying batons and, more menacingly, Kalashnikov rifles. They looked at me on my scooter and then looked at each other. Again I got the sense that they were thinking, "Where does this fool think he's going and how has he gotten this far?"

"Boarding Pass?"

"Here you go."

"Your bike can't go on the plane, sir."

"I'm sorry you're mistaken; I've just had this chat with the airline and they say it can."

"It won't fit through our x-ray machine so it can't go on the plane."

Well, that was new one. I'd not had that line before.

"Why does it need to be x-rayed? It has never been x-rayed before."

"No x-ray, no travel."

It became clear that the guy wasn't looking for a conversation around the issue.

"It collapses into different parts," I said.

"OK, do that. And put each piece on the machine."

"I'll need help to do that as I am disabled."

"I can't touch the bike until it has been x-rayed."

How very fucking convenient, I thought. Once again, I was aware of every pair of eyes in the terminal building looking at the mad Englishman arguing the toss with India's Army. It was a horrible experience.

I made my way towards a plastic seat, the type I struggle to get out of. The situation was going from bad to worse. I got off the scooter and sat on the seat. I knew straightaway that I was going to need help to get out of the seat but I had to sit down in order to dismantle the scooter. I felt an overwhelming sense of isolation and vulnerability. My independence had gone, I was now completely reliant on someone that I didn't know to help get me out of the chair. This was just the worst for me, there were no friendly faces, just a thousand pair of eyes, all looking at the disabled guy trying to get his scooter on the plane.

You could see that many of them were questioning why the disabled guy was on his own in an airport with nobody to help. The fact that independence and dignity is everybody's right, just feels lost in India. I felt incredibly vulnerable and like some sort of freak.

I started to take the scooter to bits. It became obvious to my Army friend that there was no way that I was going to be able to carry each component over to the x-ray machine. I tried to get out of the chair but as I put my weight through it as I pushed up, it moved. My legs gave way and I fell. My humiliation was complete. I felt pathetic. Face down on the floor in Delhi Airport with my scooter, my means of independence, in bits alongside me. My dignity had gone, I was angry, frustrated and ready to lash out. I was determined to try and keep calm. I was screaming inside but would not let those watching, see.

Eventually, a member of the public came to help me. Once I was off the floor, I was helped over to the exit side of the x-ray machine so that when the scooter came through, I could reassemble it and be on my way. As the different bits came through, the soldier who watched me struggle taking it apart came over and offered to help put it back together. It turned out that now it had cleared the x-ray scan and it was safe to touch, he was happy to help. Did he really think I was sitting on my own bomb?

I have never been so happy to take my seat on a plane – what an experience. I was physically and emotionally shattered. I'd never felt so vulnerable and alone as I had done in that airport. A few hours later, I was in my hotel room in Mumbai.

I collapsed on my bed. I needed a nice cold beer so I was about to head to the bar but I thought I'd bang a tweet out first. I grabbed my phone and wrote something like, "Thanks Delhi Airport for stripping me of my dignity, turns out travelling with a disability in India is not so easy" – or something like that. I pressed send and forgot all about it. The two beers I had that night before bed were the most refreshing I've ever tasted.

Two nights later and I'd just finished dinner in the hotel restaurant, I receive a call from one of ECB's Media Managers back at Lord's, Ben Walker.

"Ian, is everything alright over there?"

"Yeah, why what's up?"

"I'm going to send you something, call me back once you've seen it."

A file arrives via email.

It's a copy of the front page of the Asian Age Newspaper with the headline:

"UK Cricket Official upset over treatment at Delhi Airport."

Accompanied by a picture of the Peter Kay character Brian Potter from Phoenix Nights.

It immediately became apparent what had happened. Many of the people who know me, particularly those within disability cricket circles, call me Potter after the aforementioned character. Probably something to do with me riding around on a wheelchair all day. There's a lot of us from the north who love the series and can recite different scenes line by line.

So, I had a picture of Brian Potter in his wheelchair as my Twitter profile picture. A journalist had seen the tweet, made a story out of it and used the picture off my profile. I guess he wasn't to know it wasn't me.

Naturally, this cracked everybody up. We found it completely hilarious. I sent a copy of the front page of the paper to my dad via email as I thought he'd find it funny. Bad move.

Next night I get a call from my Mum who was panicking because my dad had seen something on the internet that suggested that I had been molested at the airport by Peter Kay, You couldn't make it up.

Slippy Floors and Hot Balls

In May 2019, I was invited out to India by the All India Cricket Association for the Physically Challenged. I developed a great relationship with these guys over the years and they'd invited me out to see how their trials and selection was developing prior to them selecting an Indian Team to participate in the 2019 Physical Disability World Series in Worcester.

I was hosted by a great bloke in Suresh Iyer, whom I'd known for a few years through his involvement in Blind Cricket in the Mumbai area. Suresh met me at Mumbai airport and escorted me to the hotel that they had sorted for me in the financial district, not too far from the airport.

The room they'd booked me was stunning and very big. It was really impressive, however the first thing I look for when entering a hotel room is the bathroom suite. Sadly, in this room, despite its luxury and its billing as an accessible room, the toilet had no handrails and there was a bath and not a wet room. I mentioned this to Suresh and in no time at all, a porter was in the room with a set of keys. He opened a locked door which we had assumed led to an adjoining room. It actually led to a huge accessible wet room. It was perfect. Handrails, a seat in the shower, and a toilet with handrails that I could reach. Magnificent, I thought and looked forward to my post-flight shower.

The only downside I could see in this bathroom were the marble walls and floor that become extremely slippery with condensation and water after a shower. There were also no handrails along the wall that led from the shower to the carpeted floor of the hallway – my non-slip sanctuary. Not to worry, if I placed towels on the floor where I would walk, and dried my hands properly before using them to balance me whilst I walked along the wall, I'd be fine.

I had one of the best post-flight showers I'd ever had, it was awesome and so refreshing. My transit from shower to lounge area started well. I'd made it halfway across the floor when my right foot slipped a bit on the towel that I had laid down. I was now positioned like a limpet/starfish facing the wall, hands apart, just above head and my feet now slightly too far apart. To drag my right

185

foot back into position, I needed to transfer my weight to my left foot, which in turn slipped away from me under the weight transfer. From being completely relaxed and comfortable, I now knew I was in trouble.

The strain on my groin was becoming painful. I couldn't move for fear of falling, I couldn't right myself and was stuck up against the wall. My feet started slipping further and further apart, I was going into a splits position and I felt my left groin tear as I slipped down the wall and my feet went further away from me. It was so painful. I looked behind me and saw that if I just fell backwards, I should land between the toilet and the sink unit and my head should miss the wall. The pain was too much in my legs and I had to get out of this position, even if falling backwards carried so much more risk of serious injury if I misjudged it.

Down I went. My head banged on the marble floor but it wasn't as bad as it could have been, and at least my legs were now in a more comfortable position although both were in spasm. I was lying on the floor looking upwards at the plumbing work under the sink. The effort of staying upright had exhausted me and being on the floor I could easily have slept. What a way to start the trip. I felt very vulnerable and alone again. The fact that I was naked didn't help, it kind of enhanced the feeling of vulnerability. I remember lying there thinking that I'd fallen in much worse bathrooms than this one. It was very nice.

I stayed on the floor for about 30 minutes, absolutely exhausted. I then decided that I needed to do something to get out of the predicament that I found myself in. I started to crawl towards the door. I realised that I'd been on the floor for so long that the floor had now dried, and now that I needed it to be a bit slippy, it was anything but.

I got to the bathroom door which was shut. It was one of those doors that closed themselves, probably to stop the steam from the bathroom setting off the fire alarm in the hallway. Thankfully, it hadn't clicked shut and I was able to get my fingers behind it to open it. This was incredibly difficult and painful for someone with very poor core stability and weakness in the arms and fingers. Every time I opened it, it closed on me before I could move through it.

I was determined that I would make it to the side of my bed and call for help from the phone beside my bed. I was also determined that I would somehow find something to cover my modesty before help arrived. I opened the door for about the 10th time and forced it wide enough for me to flop onto my shoulder so that at least when it closed again, it would hit me and I'd be a quarter of the way through it.

I crawled to the side of my bed. I had carpet burns where you really don't need carpet burns and the carpet gripper had cut my toes so I'd left a small trail of blood between the bathroom and my bed. By this time I just didn't care. I just needed someone to get me off the floor and into my bed. I managed to sit up and rest my back and head on the side of the bed. There was a towel at the end of the bed which I used to protect my dignity and save the eyes of my rescuers from being face to face with little Ian.

10 minutes later help arrived. Unfortunately, little Ian decided he wasn't gonna miss out and made an unwanted appearance, but frankly I just didn't care by that point. At least he was clean as I'd had a shower. I felt embarrassed, humiliated and stripped of any dignity. It's a horrible but recurring feeling in these situations.

It's the most undignified thing that I experience. I don't deal well with needing other people's help and it is one of the battles that I have in dealing with what is happening to my body.

In this example, I thought I had taken every precaution possible to ensure that I would be safe. Every time that I think I'm in control of this horrible condition, it comes back and bites me on the backside.

The following day, the inside of my left thigh was so bruised it looked like someone had smeared blackcurrant jam from my groin down to my knee. It was so painful. I explained to Suresh what had happened and from nowhere a tube of Deep Heat materialised. "Brilliant! I'll give that a try," I said.

The next day we had a flight to catch down to Hubli, a short flight south from Mumbai. Getting on and off those small twin-engined, turbo prop planes was an experience. They boarded me last, grace and dignity were virtues that weren't held in any esteem whatsoever when compared with the need to get the disabled guy on the plane. How I wasn't injured during these manoeuvres I'm not sure, but all's well that ends well.

We got to the hotel in Hubli, it was stunning, right on the side of a large lake. I got to my room and immediately stripped down to apply some Deep Heat to my troublesome left groin and thigh. I remember thinking that I need to apply this stuff with caution. The affected area was very close to my meat and two veg and the last thing I needed was Deep Heat on my bollocks.

I'm not sure what happened or how it happened but I got the application of the cream very wrong. Somehow, the cream managed to find my testicles. Within minutes, my balls were on fire.

I'd been in my room no more than 15 minutes and I found myself dangling my balls in a pint of cold water. I felt very much that since I'd arrived in India, I'd morphed into Mr Bean.

I relayed the story to my Indian hosts that evening, much to their amusement.

Stumps

Dad has been in the nursing home for nearly three years. In that time, he has been completely bed-bound. He has lost all control of his life and relies solely on the nurses and carers at the home to look after him.

The lockdown because of coronavirus made things even more difficult. Paul, myself and Uncle Kenny would visit each week but lockdown stopped all that. Dad couldn't grasp the reality of life outside of his room. He still thought we were living a normal life. Dad was phoning me every day, to either demand supplies or to generally have a moan about the nurses. One day he called me, asking for a diary. He said he needed a diary so that he could record the days when his bed pad was changed because he was convinced that the nurses were using the pads that we supplied for Dad, on other patients. They were billing Dad but he didn't think he was getting the use of the pads. This was typical of how Mum and Dad had been over recent years, they always seemed to think that people were ripping them off, that there was some conspiracy against them. The more rational mine or Paul's explanations were for certain things, the more upset and angry they used to get. It was draining.

On the morning of 2nd July 2020, I was getting ready to attend a meeting via Zoom regarding Blind Cricket. My phone rang and it was Dad. We spoke for 10 minutes about Everton's victory over Leicester the night before. He then told me that a Dr had been to see him the day before and had told Dad that he may have Colon Cancer. They'd found an abnormality in a blood test that suggested Colon Cancer, but they couldn't confirm it without Dad going into Wrexham Hospital for a colonoscopy.

"There's no way I'm going there," he said. "Why should I leave this safe environment to go to a hospital that's full of Covid?" It was difficult to argue against his point. His attitude was one of resignation, "If I've got cancer, I've got cancer," he said. He talked a lot about wanting to die, he'd had enough of life.

He had spoken previously about wanting to commit suicide and had also asked me to get him the details of the Dignitas Clinic in Switzerland where voluntary euthanasia is practiced. I found these conversations really upsetting. I felt as if my relationship with my parents had vanished years ago. They had caused me so much upset over so many different things and in the end, I learnt that I needed to look after myself for the sake of my own family. My mental health was taking a real battering.

I'd learned to deal with what I now accept was grief at the loss of our relationship and be comfortable with it, but the months before Mum died brought it all back again. Whilst Mum's passing was a relief, Dad's situation was very different and in many ways, much sadder.

Paul and I had offered Mum and Dad all kinds of help, advice and support over the years, all of which they declined. They fell out with Social Services; nothing was ever right for them. The bottom line in all of this was that they both had capacity to make their own decisions. As one Occupational Therapist told me, they have the capacity to make wrong decisions, the point is, they are free and able to make them.

Dad was always in control and Mum would never do anything for herself that she thought would upset Dad. Dad called the shots and Mum was quite submissive. That was the way their marriage worked, they were happy. Who am I to judge what is right and wrong? They were both really opinionated, and God help you if you didn't agree with them. There was no give and take and no grey areas – everything was black and white. Whatever the Daily Mail said was gospel. No matter what experience of an issue Paul or I had, if the Daily Mail said otherwise, then there was no changing their position on anything.

So back to the nursing home. Dad had lost his wife, carer and best friend 18 months ago. The one person whom he could order around and expect to deliver whatever he asked for, had departed. He was realising that this generation of females are better able to stand up for themselves and in the case of the nurses are also extremely busy looking after more people than just Dad.

He has lost control and it must be devastating for him because he is now so alone and dependent on others. But the people he is now dependent on have other responsibilities, of which, he is but one. I can't imagine what it must be like to be diagnosed with a condition but not wanting to be treated for it. In all honesty, even if he did want treatment I'm not sure that he'd survive it. His liver disease and diabetes have made him so weak that I don't imagine that he'd survive any of the cancer treatments.

I'm finding it hard. My father, who hasn't always been the most supportive or understanding of me and my wishes, is now phoning me every day. He doesn't ask how I am or what I've been up to, he just gives me a list of demands. My own disability is getting worse and Covid lockdown and the financial situation at ECB was causing me anxiety surrounding my job security. These are situations that I have no control over. My Dad is bed-bound on the second floor of a nursing home, we can't even see him through a window. He is lying there, wanting to die and the reality is that we might not ever see him again.

I'm not sure that any of us deserve what is happening.

Despite some of the difficulties that life has thrown at me, I feel very lucky to have led the life that I have. None of us know when our time to depart will come. In my view, we should all try and cram as much into our lives as possible. Recognise that others have had different experiences to you and that you can learn from everybody whom you meet. Respect differences and value those who think differently to you. A variation from the norm is a point of difference and a potential strength. It gives a different perspective and a set of experiences that will make a collective more representative.

Resilience and the ability to manage whatever life throws at you is a major strength and most disabled people have it in abundance. They have to in order to deal with the crap that they face on a daily basis. I'm not disabled by whatever disease it is that I have. I am a functioning adult and I use my Powerchair to mitigate the impact of the condition that I have. I become disabled when the solutions that I have found to manage my illness are met with mostly man-made barriers. I don't feel disabled until I find I can't access someone's house or I can't access a shop or a building.

I wish I could say that I don't get frustrated with my physical deterioration. It seems that every day now, something reminds me that I'm not what I was. Tying shoelaces, buttoning shirts and trousers, using a knife and fork, getting in and out of bed, the struggles often get the day off to a very average start.

Paul Cartwright, a humble volunteer from Wrexham, changed my life. Or rather, he gave me the opportunity to make decisions that would change my life. The bottom line is that without him, my story would be very different.

I have so much to thank the sport of cricket for, I owe it so much. Cricket has provided me with a purpose, it has enabled me to accept my limitations and deal with an impairment that sometimes makes me cry with frustration. I just cannot imagine what my or my family's life would be like without cricket.

191

Disability Cricket became my purpose and the focus of my professional life and I hope that I have made a difference.

I have found that rather than limiting my life, the condition that I have has enabled me to make choices that have enhanced my existence. In some ways, that is quite a selfish thing to say. I am sure that Joanna and my children would love to see me able to climb stairs or join them on different trips that are inaccessible to me in my Powerchair. I'm sure they would love to see me walking without needing to hold on to furniture for balance. As my condition deteriorates, it is becoming easier to slip into thinking that life is about my needs – it certainly isn't. The hardest thing about living with a deteriorating condition is seeing the impact it has on Jo and the children. Their resilience, support and understanding has enabled me to live my best life. The very least that I can do for them is to keep living it for as long as I can.

Epilogue

Writing this memoir has been cathartic and therapeutic. It has helped me find context and relive memories both good and bad. To clarify, Joanna has never really forgiven me for welcoming her home from hospital with a soaking wet mattress. Although we can talk about it now without me having to leave the room for fear of being slapped. Conor understands that he had to be an Evertonian, there was no choice, it's just how it is.

And just so you are sure, I was NOT the Phantom Shitter on board Ark Royal.

And the mustard bumming pants never saw the light of day again.

I hope that you have found that I have been honest and open in sharing my experiences. That was my intention. There will be things that you might have handled differently to how I did. That's my point really, we are all different and we all have our own perceptions and views of the world and ways of dealing with the things that life throws at us.

Conor and Ciara are now young adults and starting to make their own way in life. It amazes me how two children from the same gene pool can be so different. Conor is so laid-back, he is horizontal. The way he has coped with his dyslexia is amazing. I look at him and admire his quiet determination and his easy-going nature – definitely his mother's son. Ciara is the polar opposite. Driven, determined and fiercely independent. She knows what she wants and goes and gets it. I always said that when she brings her first boyfriend home, I'd sit him down and tell him how things were going to be in terms of his relationship with my daughter. I now imagine that I will shake his hand, wish him luck and tell him I'm here to talk if he needs to. She's a beautiful and formidable young lady.

In terms of my diagnosis, I am still waiting for investigations to be concluded that will hopefully establish what neurological condition I have. With CMT, there was a 50/50 chance that my children could inherit it. I now don't know what to tell them and that is the hardest part.

More than ever, I am convinced that the injections that I was given whilst in the Gulf have impacted on my genetic make-up. I accept that I had the defective CMT gene passed down from my father but difference in how we have both been affected is marked. At the age of 50, Dad was still able to walk the half mile, up and down a hill, to our local. I have to hold on to furniture and balance on walls to walk from my bedroom to the toilet, and more often than not, I use a Powerchair in the house now.

Dad is 25 years older than me and has been completely bed-bound for three years in the same room in a nursing home. If I deteriorate to that level, I don't know what I would do. It frightens the life out of me if I sit and think about it. But then, for some reason, I don't feel that outcome is meant for me. I don't see my days ending in a nursing home. In private moments, in the safety of my own home or when I'm in a hotel room, I think about how I might end up. I think that diabetes or complications arising from it will ultimately see me off. I just hope that happens before I lose all independence.

As I mentioned earlier, the real torment for me is the impact on my children. I can't tell them anything at the moment with any certainty. I just hope that should they inherit the condition from me, that they also are able to muster up some of the strength that I've needed to deal with it.

There's no point in me being bitter about anything – it won't cure the pain or frustration. An accurate diagnosis would help and if the MoD do have an element of culpability, then an acknowledgement and apology would go a long way. I have no desire to go through the courts for compensation. Money cannot solve the damage that has been done. Besides, I reckon there are plenty of people that have plenty of money but have not been as happy as I have been in my life.

Many of the barriers that need to be overcome by people with a physical disability are still prevalent. I still encounter disabled toilets used as store cupboards and lifts filled with boxes. I get asked if I've got a license for my Powerchair several times a day when I am out and about and if I'm holding a pint, I'll get a comment about drink driving. Air travel remains a nightmare and so family holidays abroad have ended because the cost of Business Class seat for me is well out of our price range. We are still an under-represented sector of society on boards and committees, and too many people seem to know what's best for us without consulting us. We will never achieve cultural change in terms of inclusion until decision-making forums are fully representative. When over 20% of the population has a long-term health issue, what on earth is the rest of the population thinking when we still need "awareness" training? It's about respecting differences in each other, and if we need to be trained regarding how to respect others then I think we have bigger issues than we think.

I'm still working at ECB and for the most part, enjoying my role. Writing the book has made me realise how far the disabled game has come and how many amazing people I have had the pleasure to work with. I still have the ambition to see cricket as the number one non-Paralympic team sport in the world and I believe that it is achievable, but sadly as a sport, we remain some way off that pinnacle. It is a major cause of frustration and people with disability the world over deserve more in this day and age.

As a cricket lover/badger, I have been fortunate that the sport has given me amazing opportunities and memories that will last a lifetime. Joanna and I have been to Buckingham Palace twice and met the Queen. I've dined in the Long Room at Lord's and had my name printed in Wisden – these are things that I never thought would happen to me growing up as a cricket loving kid. I became a member of MCC in 2012 and I take my place at the front of the Warner Stand for a couple of days at each Test Match. I was able to take Conor to the 2019 World Cup final, what a day that was.

I've been a member of the Lord's Taverners since 2008 and a Trustee since 2017. The Tavs are the country's leading sports charity supporting disabled and disadvantaged youngsters. The charity does amazing work and I'm proud that ECB and the Lord's Taverners have recently signed a partnership that sees both organisations working together to deliver a grassroots disability cricket program called Super 1's.

As much as cricket has given me, I want to give back. As I mentioned earlier, you lead to serve. During the summer of 2020 when so much cricket was lost because of the Covid-19 Pandemic, I was really proud to see members of the England Physical Disability team step forward and fundraise for the Taverners, with Captain Callum Flynn stating that they wanted to provide the opportunity for youngsters with a disability to follow in their footsteps.

I'm proud to have played a part in giving these lads a platform to develop their talent and to make their mark.

I am also a Trustee at the Neuro-Muscular Centre (NMC) in Winsford in Cheshire. The centre provides physio and other holistic support for people with neuro-muscular conditions such as my own. The care and support that I have received there over the last 16 years has been exceptional. It's as much about the psychological support of having people to talk to as it is about the physiotherapy sessions. I'd never spoken to anyone outside of my family who had CMT before I went there.

The staff have been central to my wellbeing and understanding of the condition.

So, here I am, at the end of my book. I hope you have enjoyed it. I hope that I have told an interesting story. There is so much more to tell, particularly on the cricketing side of things but that is for another time. For now, I can put the laptop away and know that I've told my story, in my words, and say that I'm proud to be different and to give a voice to disabled cricketers the world over.

You can play cricket in a wheelchair and I hope that I've contributed to make that a possibility for many more people.

Appendices

I'd like to recognise here some of the people who have made a significant contribution to supporting my work at ECB and disability cricket generally.

Pete Ackerley Martin Dean Gary Bass
Pete Edmondson Chris Porter John Cook
Bobby Denning Ross Hunter Ron Young
Ian Powell Blyth Duncan Derek Morgan
Kate Peckham Fran Clarkson Gary Metcalfe
Jason Bowen Les Randall Ian Leather
Emma Foden Pete Sugg Chris Highton
Mike Hutchinson Neil Bradshaw Richard Hill
Will Kitchen Dayle Stancliffe Chris Ellison
Qasim Ali Phil Hudson Paul Box-Grainger
Tom Flowers Stuart Murphy. Lauren Hopper
Ben Walker Paul Bedford Mike Gatting
Gordon Hollins Hugh Morris Paul Downton
Ashley Giles Steve Elworthy Edgar Herridge
Bill Higginson Mike O'Mahoney David Lloyd
Dave Gavrilovic Ian Salisbury James Kirtley
Nicky Pemberton Henry Hazlewood Mark Bond
BACD ECAD BCEW CFPD Stefan Pichowski
Scott Gormley George Camm Martyn Kiel
Graham Redfern Louise Croft Rachel Atkinson
Richard Olejar Ben Langley Anjali Bamrah
Peter Dixon Nigel George Sula Gleeson Tim Shutt
Alison Faiers Dave Leighton

Also the countless Super 1's development officers and Table Cricket coaches up and down the country.

Of course, the problem with this sort of list is that there will always be someone that may feel disappointed that I've missed them off the list. So I'll just say a huge thank you to everyone who has been on the journey.

Overseas Tours Led by Ian Martin

2008   England Blind to Australia

2009   England Learning Disability to Australia

2010   England Blind to Sharjah

2011   England Deaf to Australia
        England Learning Disability to South Africa
        England Physical Disability to Dubai

2012   England Blind to India

2013   England Deaf to South Africa

2014   England Physical Disability to Dubai

2014   England Blind to South Africa

2015   England Learning Disability to Australia
        England Physical Disability to Bangladesh

2016   England Blind to Australia
        England Physical Disability to Dubai

2017. England Blind to India

2018   England Blind to India

2019   England Learning Disability to Australia

Overseas First-Class Cricket Venues Visited

St John's Recreation Ground, Antigua
Sir Vivian Richards Stadium, Antigua
Stanford Cricket Ground, Antigua
GABBA, Brisbane, Australia
SCG, Sydney, Australia
MCG, Melbourne, Australia
WACA, Perth, Australia
Allan Border Fields, Albion, Australia
Manuka Oval, Canberra, Australia
Bradman Oval, Bowral Australia
Traeger Park, Alice Springs, Australia
North Sydney Oval, Australia
Junction Oval, St Kilda, Australia
Mirpur, Dhaka, Bangladesh
Kensington Oval, Barbados
Three W's Oval, Barbados
ICC Academy, UAE
Dubai Cricket Stadium, UAE
Sharjah Cricket Stadium, UAE
Wankhede, Mumbai, India
Brabourne Stadium, Mumbai, India
Chinnaswammy, Bangalore, India
Cricket Club of India, Mumbai, India
Wanderers, South Africa
De Beers Diamond Oval, Kimberley, South Africa
Mamalode, South Africa
Newlands, South Africa

Boland Park, South Africa
Centurion, South Africa
Queens Park Oval, Trinidad
Brian Lara Stadium, Trinidad

Ian's All-Time Disability XI

1. Umesh Valjee   MBE   Deaf
2. Chris Edwards   Learning Disability
3. Dan Bowser   Learning Disability
4. Callum Flynn   Physical Disability
5. Jamie Goodwin   Physical Disability
6. Liam O'Brian   Physical Disability
7. Liam Thomas   Physical Disability
8. George Greenway   Deaf
9. Mark Woodman   Deaf
10. Paul Allen   Deaf
11. Tayler Young   Learning Disability
12. Matt Askin   Physical Disability

There are so many other players who could consider themselves really unlucky not to have made this list. Sorry guys, I could only pick 11 and a 12th Man.

I'm also going to indulge myself and pick a best XI from the Blind Cricketers that I have known over the years, and because it's my own list, I haven't bothered with choosing by sight category.

Ian's Blind Cricket XI

1. Justin Hollingsworth
2. Matt Dean
3. Luke Sugg
4. Dan Field
5. Pete Blueitt
6. Hassan Khan
7. Mo Khatri
8. Heindrich Swanepoel
9. Ed Hossell
10. Nathan Foy
11. Jimmy Millard